THE BRIDGE VOLUME-II

bridge-the-nations.com
pictureshowpress.net

Cover Design: Qasim Nawaz
Calligraphy: Husnain Haider Mumtaz

FIRST EDITION

ISBN-13: 978-1-7341702-4-5

THE
BRIDGE VOLUME-II

Writings by contemporary wirters from Pakistan & The United States

Editors

Aaisha Umt Ur Rashid
Shannon Phillips

CONTENTS

POEMS FROM PAKISTAN

POEMS FROM THE UNITED STATES

The Bridge: An Enchanting Marvel-land of Words

"Sitting across the blood-seeking, three-headed beast, Shehrzade had no plausible option but to obey the beast's command and tell a tale, a new one every night, for a thousand nights and one, to stay alive. So tell a story she did:
Once upon a time, long long ago..."

Storytelling, in poem or prose, comes natural to us, the homo-sapiens. We've been telling stories since the night before time immemorial in that ancient valley when our great ancestors huddled around the flaming fire and crafted the first ever story for their toddlers who, clinging to the grown-ups, shivered less of the cold night and more of the wolves howling somewhere in the dense forests up in the surrounding mountains.

Stories soothed them; so did the tunes of a lullaby, putting them to a comfortable sleep.

Since that eventful night, every culture or civilization and every region or country has nurtured its very own folklore, passed on from generations, through centuries of mythological development. Embedded in the depth of psyche, the collective literature travels and varies as we hop onto different regions of the globe. Mixing ideas from across the globe into an irresistible cocktail is what we name as an anthology: much like the one in your hands right now.

Grown out of the seeds of imagination of two nations, identical in some aspects, diverse in others; the anthology under study connects two societies that are, if sought on an atlas, many a thousand mile apart; hence the name *The Bridge*.

Being poles apart as various roots of American ways of life are compared to our own in Pakistan, it was, indeed, an amazing and, to a greater extent, a uniting experience to spot the commonalities in the roots of literature on both sides. It can thus be claimed on good authority that humanity, though spread far and wide on the planet, breathes in the same Oxygen of love, tolerance and respect. *The Bridge* provides an ample proof to the assertion.

The first country being Pakistan and second America, the cocktail offers an ethnically diverse, yet a closely interlinked montage of delicacies to a reader's word-gobbling tastebuds. Contributions by Rizwan Akhtar, Sana Munir, Zakia Nasir and Iffat Saeed, amongst many others will, in quite a free-flowing manner, unfurl the deep lines on your furrowed brow, one by one, soothing your senses as the splendor of literature washes over you. The assortment from the American side including contributions by Lloyd David Aquino, Kareem Tayyar and poems by Christina Brown and Suzanne Allen will also amuse your senses and I must say that both Aaisha Umt Ur Rashid and Shannon Phillips have picked up the right ingredients for the cocktail.

There comes a moment in reading a well-crafted piece, be it a poem or a short story, when the reader's focus must not be on speed but on the lack of it. The writings in this anthology, if you linger through them languidly, unhurried, will reveal to you a mysterious cloud of perfumery, permeating every ounce of your being.

"Unputdownable" is quite familiar jargon now for an incredible read and I wouldn't feel shy of using it for *The Bridge*.

"The night had dawned upon the bed chambers of Shehrzade, candles flickering within and the moon glowing outside. As the beast stared upon her, eagerly enough, hungry for a new story; she began unraveling, slowly, some new mysteries out of her fancy:

"Miles away from mainland Greece, there once lived an enchantress who ..."

Rehman Faris
(Poet, Writer, Columnist)

FROM THE EDITORS

Part of the fun of being the editor of such an anthology is the countless revelations you find along the way. The exposure you get to your own internal thinking patterns during such a journey is quite enlightening. Your shaky perspectives evolve, your ideas flourish and more than all that, the unlearning taking place within you throughout is worth the strife.

The project of *The Bridge*, taken as a whole, aims at connecting writers from across the globe while uniting them on one platform where they can exhibit creative pieces of timeless relevance. Each volume targets writers from one country and the work is evaluated without any societal prejudices or religious constraints. The first volume allied with the Malaysian writers while Volume-II caters writers from America. Along with bringing out the similarities, *The Bridge* accepts and highlights the cultural divergence that is exhibited through broad-based contributions. That, precisely, is the power of connectivity and the outcome is in your hands.

The Bridge (Volume-II) is a compilation of moments, expressed in prose and verse, that will reignite your faith in the power of roots that might sometimes be overlooked but can never be replicated. The anthology contains poems and stories to rally the human spirit, making us all connect through the experiences we can relate to and emotions we all undergo. With a variety of in-depth and tuneful tales to inspire you, I hope *The Bridge (Volume-II)* will be a good addition to your bookshelves.

Aaisha Umt Ur Rashid
Editor from Pakistan

When Aaisha informed me of the theme for *The Bridge (Volume-II) – roots* – the first thing I thought of was "Roots," the 1977 TV miniseries. The show follows the life of a young African man (and his descendants) who was forced into slavery in North America. My next thought was, *Wow, "roots" in the United States is a very complicated thing...* But then, I immediately chastised myself because, of course, it must also be very complex in Pakistan.

Since Aaisha and I first embarked on this project, the world has changed, and *complex* doesn't even begin to describe it. At the time of this writing, we are in the summer of 2020 and the coronavirus is still wreaking havoc everywhere. Furthermore, protests are taking place all over the world, but the ones I feel most acutely are the ones happening in my country. On May 25th, 2020, George Floyd, a Black man, died after a police officer kneeled on his neck for "eight minutes and forty-six seconds." Since that day, protests against police brutality have been ongoing in major cities across the country. Three police officers (along with several witnesses) were present to watch George Floyd die, and millions and millions of people have now seen the video(s). The whole world is watching, and writers and readers everywhere are processing the best way they know how – with stories.

I "met" Aaisha through a mutual acquaintance, Saif Islam, who has been a huge supporter of this project. It is my understanding that Saif and Aaisha know each other through a course on creative writing. I "met" Saif through another writer, Muhammad Sumili, who allowed me the privilege of publishing a collection of his short stories. Muhammad was a student at an

English language school where I worked. What is notable to me here is that the four of us are from four different countries, and we are bound together by a love of reading and writing.

I highlight these relationships because I think that Aaisha's vision and her impulse to connect writers (and readers) from different parts of the world through *The Bridge* is exactly right. Stories help us develop connections with others, and in times like these, connection is one thing that will help us get through.

Shannon Phillips
Editor from The United States

POEMS FROM PAKISTAN

Dig In | *Rizwan Akhtar*

The worst thing about vocabulary
is that it boosts a structure
a unitary territory one is averse to
then words want more recognition
so an affair between sentences
rattles nights, when a lonely heart
seeks an unlimited redress
what a travesty of all allusions!
carefully planted in conversations
either over a cup of coffee or
Derridean deconstruction, always
meant to rupture the established
canon of love to stratify its
imperial command we follow
therefore sentences become
passages which deteriorate
like graves in cemeteries and
sooner or later even epithets
crack, underneath a skeleton
of a poem reveals a history
of digging (Not that of Heaney's)
but a raw animal scrapping of
the soil hence a script comes
where silence rules innocently.

The Diaspora Hankerings | *Zakia Nasir*

As I stood under the profusely blossoming trees
The huge clusters nearly fanning my face
with their feathery soft petals and laden branches
I looked around.
The trees lined both sides of the wet concrete road
darkened by intermittent rain adding a chill to the wind,
which strewed blossom petals lining the pavement
adding a pink hue to the asphalt grey of the road.
What's the name of these blossom trees I mused?
My diaspora friend looked blankly at me.
Ambivalence evident in her frown as she concentrated to think
    up the name
She had never given a thought to nature
having been planted in a land away from her roots.
A land too strange for her to negotiate.

I remembered the names on trees along the canal in Lahore.
Yes! and in Lawrence garden, as fireflies fluttered in my memory
In warm summer eves we gathered them in our frocks
to lighten our bed canopies on hot summer nights.
Here they would die of cold I thought.
Just as the warmth of memories have died of cold in some
under the burden of survival.
But memories do surface time and again they tell me
when the hearts saddened by distance and despair
longed for the lost homelands of yore
longed for the smell of their soil.
Diaspora longings cut at their guts
They know they have lost their homes forever
deceived by madness for greener pastures.

Never can they now taste the nectars of lost springs
Never can lost homelands of youth be regained
Never again can they be joined to the cut off roots
I look around alarmed
Was I to be one of them?
I saw
Men and women trudged past
shoulders hunched to the whistling wind
breathing deep sighs of longing.
They furtively eyed the still freshness of my expectations
My bemused wonder at beauteous nature
I was still ignorant of the wintry cold dark depressive long evenings,
They thought!
When radiators fail to warm dead hopes and cold bodies
The old time hearths at least ignited flames of desire
dead now in chilly wintry nights.
Secretly musing my heart sank!
I'll be one day regretting like them
Hankerings of return clawing my heart.
But no!
Though I empathize their diaspora longings
Though I pity their helplessness
I know I've come to go back
I know I will go back one day!

Let Me Be | *Iffat Saeed*

Sing to me the song of nightingale
The murmur of mermaids at sea
Ease me out of this mortal pain
The anguish of despair
Bring me the vine of opium and
A platter
Of Manna dew
Take away my pain and give me the delectable
Dhool a Pak
O Sheikh heed my paean and seep into me
Spin me on my axis
Whirl me away
To the land of my beloved
Carry me to the firmament
Allow me a crevice... an oracle
Metamorphise me in stupor and
In ecstasy
Loose the coil
Unlock the grid
Free me
Melt the frieze and
Let me be...

Ebony of My Life! | *Saima Eman*

Living in the world of life!
My roots, my race, my ebony!
Differ we may over this or that!
Made we are of water and clay!
I eat, I feel, I sleep
And so do you!
You are the animal, I love,
You are the plant, I gain from!
You are the earth, I live on,
You are the human, I converse with!
I need what you need,
You are for me and I am for you,
In harmony with you and your harmony with me
Blessed we are, blessed we would be!
One day, I drilled a hole in you, a deep unfailing wound!
You suffered, lingered, and passed on,
And finally, I received a hole, the same deep unfailing wound!
That devoured me! Devouring life, devouring the world!
It didn't end there and then!
The wounds bled till death,
One life story end bred another one!
Sigh! Till nothing was left!
Not even nothingness itself!
Nothingness had a reason to live!
Nothingness needed exploration, mystery, and awe!
Even, Nothingness drew inspiration from life and love!
Nah! This is not the end!
It is the warning of the end that mustn't be!
Had we cared and loved the life within us?
Had we passed the good and love?

Had we done?
Life would have nurtured and bloomed!

Like a flower splashing a fountain of colours,
Like the wind spattering wings of freedom,
Like mushrooming of a succulent crisp breeze!
Like a never-ending fairy tale with eternal lovers!
Being in love with life is the beginning
Of an end that never ends!
Care about life, why should I?
Because I am,
If life is,
And life is, when I am!
I am a living being.
My roots, my race, my ebony!

The Humanity's Tree | *Nausheen Mazhar*

Roots of Humanity's tree grew deep
Only its branches spread in 'East' and 'West'
'Flowers' of different shades blossomed on it,
And nurtured love in its very nest!
But as time passed, things began to change
And Humanity was no longer at its very best!
Differences, rivalries, animosity and hate
Pushed it to a level as loathsome as a pest!
Slavery, war, honor killing... thus hatred started to prevail
Still the roots remained bounded, bridging 'East to the 'West'!!!

Tracing My Roots | *Zakia Nasir*

My roots go deep down in my land where I was born
They spread towards the land of my parent's origin
Leading to those ancient times when man was born
I am Adam's child daughter of Eve
The revered man whom I do not blame for being tempted
This was so ordained
God made this world for man!
Beautified it with femininity
Colored it with spring
Made woman the harbinger of spring
Gave Adam control
And gave him the stronger role
We are born thus from courage and beauty
Our roots lie embedded in both
We continued to live and branch out
We created traditions and we gave the world life
My roots are thus everywhere!
But I like giving names
I like assigning heroic roles to my antecedents
I stand united with the human kind
With them I share common goals and aims
Though oceans apart we at heart are the same
We have the same roots
Same struggles same aspirations, same goals
We share ideals of humanity and posterity
Our roots are thus visionary
Based on inspired humanism
Human roots we are the same.

Brown │ *Areej Tahir*

Some time ago, I told you,
That you remind me of brown,
An explanation is long overdue,
Why don't you sit down?

To the world, brown is dull,
But to me, brown is underrated,
Undervalued by the owners of thick, hollow skulls,
Who cares about people with opinions so outdated?

First of all, let me make it clear,
You are too precious to be just a single color,
You are numerous shades of brown, my dear,
Like a day of mild, warm, happy summer,

When someone drowns in an ocean,
And saline water fills his lungs,
But somehow struggles his way up by great devotion,
You are the brown shore that he hugs,

Or when the sky pours down relentlessly,
Or when the sun scorches every living being,
It is the strong brown land that stands tall, splendidly,
It is the brown sand that glistens, beaming,

You are the soft brown shore line,
You are the wise brown tree trunk,
To me, you are a life line,
Deep inside me, your essence has sunk,

Oh so when someone asks you what you are,
Tell them you are just like the brown land,
That gives rise to all the exotic colors there are,
The constant support to help you when you stand,

The ignored, unnoticed brown,
That doesn't need anyone else's attention,
Because you are too strong to be brought down,
Because you are present in every dimension.

Yearning for Change | *Areej Tahir*

As juvenile hearts are murdered in cold blood,
As massacred innocence floods the underlying mud,
As the preachers of brutality pluck all the precious floral buds,
My heart yearns for change,

As chaste, naïve adolescents are tainted,
As their fragile bodies are bought and rated,
As their souls are manipulated, contaminated, intoxicated,
My heart yearns for change,

As people are kept illiterate to preserve ignorance,
For wakefulness can cause a major hindrance,
Because corruption is the only product at their end of deliverance,
My heart yearns for change,

As in every inch of the street, a different sect resides,
As the conflicting opinion of the ministers of the same religion
    divides,
As during the month of Muharram, it's not safe to go outside,
My heart yearns for change,

As families leave for merely a stroll,
But return in shreds, devoid of souls,
As in a split second green lands turn into dust bowls,
My heart yearns for change,

As for the sins of men, sacrificed are the little girls and their big
    futures,

Because in the form of landlords and judges exist disguised vultures,
And this crime conveys the true essence of the chaotic culture,
My heart yearns for change,

As people die of starvation, new roads are being paved,
As people expire due to filthy water, new train stations are
    being made,
As help is commercialized, but nobody actually comes to aid,
My heart years for change,

As our fellowmen are begging for support and refuge,
As they drown in the metallic deluge,
We stay silent because our debts to their enemies are huge,
My heart yearns for change,

As the rich crimes are abated by distractions and silently buried,
As children die because they were too many and malnourished,
As the flame of the flickering candle is diminished,
My heart yearns for change.

POEMS FROM
THE UNITED STATES

A Fortiori | *Patty Seyburn*

The vines must suffer
in order to produce

good wine, he said,

versus the vines suffer
because they must, and

incidentally

produce good wine – when
the vines don't suffer

(by law, no longer required –
irrigation no longer taboo,

the primacy of rain water,
disputed)

will quality suffer? What suffers
is perception:

suffering necessary,
and watering the vines will

produce more grapes
but worse wine (a case of

verschlimmbesserung – improvements
bring unforeseen problems –

– unless

this is not true at all
and centuries of arid

soil and deprivation,
"stressing the vines"

while keeping down
the water bill,

did not contribute to
the quality of wine. What to do

with beliefs debunked?
My favorite

atheist smiles: let's drink
this two-buck-chuck

and I reach for a bottle
of Chateau

Something – what am I
saving it for? My palate shocked

by years of Egri Bikaver
(Bull's Blood), Bud

Lite and margaritas made
with Lemon-X sour cocktail mix.

As for the connection
between making art and

suffering, please
quit telling me I have not

suffered enough – you have no
idea – I mean, really, you have

no idea, you
have no – do these

plums taste good to you? They grow
on trees.

Voiced and Unvoiced: Resumed Litany
for All Language | *Judy Kronenfeld*

And blessed be the wholly ghostly psychological reality
of the phoneme which maketh there to be a difference
between *sit* and *zit* in English (though not in my parents'
immigrant kitchen) and whose oil has burned
– lo! these millennia –
lighting the ways of the tongue.

Blessed be the *mama-loshn* of my forefathers and my foremothers,
wet as coffee shpritzed from mother's good-mood
mouth when papa made a joke in her mid-sip,
throaty as catarrh, dentalized as Brooklyn –
Yiddish – streaked with Hebrew – departing the world,
        departing the room
of my life with my departed parents, but whose *sillage*
is a complex of distillation of newly dug
potatoes still clotted with clumps
of earth, natural essence of chopped
onion, and a *soupçon* of vapor of crackling
chicken fat.

Blessed be the singing correction, *une a l'ancienne-NUH!*
of Madame in the boulangerie just down the street
from our old hotel, as she hands me
the bread of my quickening life, above the ground,
in the Tuileries – a warm baguette with crispy horns.

And blessed be all the dancing languages of voice
and tone, in touch with other voices
and tones – even those of the man holding the door

for that extra pulse
when I am nanoseconds behind
the usual door-holding distance, so that I gratefully hurry my steps
and my *Merci!* registers a mite
of pleased surprise, as well as appreciation,
and his nod and *"Pas de quoi,"* the tiniest
noblesse oblige.

Oh blessed be the layryngeals, glottal stops,
the clicks and high/low tones,
all the word-engendering differences in the thousand
lexicons I do not know, that create chitchat-chew-the-fat-confab
rattling across the breathing globe – like the difference
between *gyà* (in my anthropologist spouse's Fanti dictionary,
"to guide") and *gya* (apparently, "to forsake"), though the tones
talk only to those raised with a taste for *fufu* and *kenke,*
and an ear tuned to the goat-skinned African drum.

Blessed be these musics that have entered
my one good ear, and blessed be
the ear, and, if need be, blessed
be the silence.

And blessed be the thoughts I think in silence
of my dead parents
and blessed be their silence
and blessed be their memories
Zikhronam Livrachah
May their memories be for a blessing.

Eating at Home | *Aruni Wijesinghe*

for my mother, who feeds me

As old as I may get
I still revert to my childhood definition
of home, the house where my family lives,
where I am still young
and dependent on the group
to define who I am
in the wide world. Home
is where my name
comes as natural as words
like *safe* and *sky*,
school and *blue* and *dinner*.
Home is the roundness of vowels,
names with meanings that tie me back
to an island lush
with groves of cinnamon trees,
breadfruit, coconut palms.
Home is the warmth of afternoon sunlight
that I can drink, warmth of cardamom,
floral and familiar,
coriander and cumin
like dust and smoke and ash.

Home is plates of rice and *dhal*,
the taste of curries and gravies
dyed sienna with roasted curry powder,
afternoon sun yellow of turmeric,
and my mother's voice
asking me if I want
more okra, more chutney.

Home is the smell of food that lingers
on my fingertips only here, at home,
where I am secure enough
to eat with my fingers, sink
into the full sensory experience
of truly eating,
the tactile joys of rice and curry,
where I am not separated from my meals
with fork and spoon.

These meals I will slowly learn
to replicate in my own kitchen,
following notes written
in my mother's flowing, tidy hand.
Recipe instructions are incomprehensible
with measurements of palm-ful and dash,
except I have witnessed her prepare
a procession of these meals over my lifetime
at home.

In the slanting afternoon sun
seeping in through half-closed blinds
we drink tea, not like the English,
but with teaspoons
of sweetened condensed milk,
the names Borden or Carnation peeping
out of the cupboard above the electric teapot,
next to Tupperware containers
of loose-leaf tea from Champika's tea estate,

or if we are feeling lazy, tea bags, never Lipton's,
but Dilmah, which we have to buy across town
in Artesia from the few shelves
at Pioneer Cash and Carry
that stock the groceries and brands
we use to make the meals
we eat at home.

912 South Fourth Street, #5 | *Suzanne Allen*

after Donna Hilbert

I was born in a valley –
foothills looming and
beaches beckoning –
I never wondered if I'd stay
or leave. My dreams
were of love
or so I thought. Freeways
unfurled like red carpets
in every direction.

In Alhambra, California
I am not yet nine months old.
My father leans over my crib
as the earth trembles –
some minor fault line slips,
rippling through our geography.
This, his memory, grounds
me, paints us in proximity –
always calls me home.

Legacy | *Patty Seyburn*

The reason Lot's wife turned to salt
was because she favored salt in her cooking.
As do I.
We turn to the familiar.
Had she flavored with sage or thyme,
her looking back would have rendered her
one of those spices. Plenty of herbs
in the bible: anise and balm, mint and cumin,
myrrh and mustard, cinnamon, saffron.
Of course, the famed bitter:
horehound, tansy, endive.
Lot's wife could have become
a hill of coriander,
which supposedly manna
resembled, and she would have been known
not only for regret, or for not listening to God
but also for sustenance. I would rather
die on that hill.

Muddy Waters | *Kareem Tayyar*

I should have left the house hours ago,
but his voice keeps rising
from the river of this record
like a knight in a legend I was taught in school,
one where some men can see the future,
but only the rare man can know the past.

A Study of Fear as a Houseplant | *Christina Brown*

I think my mother gave it to me and before that
her mother gave it to her
and my sister and I make a game of seeing
who can propagate the most clippings
which is to say
we make a game of seeing who is not afraid
to choose the sharpest blade to best behead the stems
who can pull what we've learned out by the roots gentle enough
and bury the living in the dirt without killing
who can keep a shadow of something else alive
and which of us can live with more ghosts.

Welsh Stone | *Mifanwy Kaiser*

It was
a stone picked up
at the seaside
in Aberystwyth

It was
the teapot and the table top

It was
Cwmbran
Cwm – valley, bran – crow
The family village
valley of the crows

It was
the chink, chink, chink
of the iceman
up the gravel driveway in winter

It was
two-inch cream
on the winter milk

It was
Christmas morning stockings
the orange in the toe, the record player, the blue two-wheeler

It was the mountain
in front of Nannie's house

far away, no rain
close up, rain

It was
Wellingtons and stomping
the rain-puddled road

It was

Welsh Cakes
and Jimmy Jones
ringing his bicycle bell
as he passed the house

It was
Grancha Button's handlebar mustache
jiggling
as he read the Sunday paper to Grannie

It was Grampi Williams
sneaking to the cupboard
for his drink

It was
the bird
with the broken wing
who flew away

It was
the tree beside Llantarnem Chapel
the graveyard

the gravestone
the grave
its bare branches the hands of the dead
reaching out to God.

When I Think of Roots | *Brian Harman*

I think of my grandparents first,
foundations of my life,
Redwood roots, Agave roots,
except for my father's biological mother,
a self-imposed root killer.
I think of my mother, uprooted
to another state by her job,
a landslide of a decision to leave California,
yet her sentimental ivy of love
long enough to extend back across
stretches of Route 66
where my dad got his kicks
from being more like a lone tobacco plant;
potted, imprisoned roots, regardless,
some of his dry soiled foundation dust
blown my way – at 66, cancer
into ashes into a Newport Harbor kelp bed,
his half-brother's roots up in the clouds,
his half-sister's roots conjured
through her "friend," the Ouija board –
I chose not to contact my father's spirit
on a rare visit to see my hemlocked
half-aunt when she asked me
what did I want to get out of visiting her.
I'm still not sure I have a wreathed answer
to suffice such a metaphysical question.
Perhaps, I was thinking, maintenance
of roots to be necessary, her being
the closest living relative to my father's
side, but some blood roots bleed out,

leading to sometimes leaving
family tree roots to the underground,
yield to roses and remembrances,
spring up beyond storied histories,
beyond the protection of mother's garden,
roots closer to that of channeled
information, influence, interpolation,
the germination of the square root,
what gets tended is generally cultivable.
I have tending of my own to do,
the roots of friends, the family field,
a new root sprung for the extended future
of my name – my roots turn gray,
my son sunkissed on the grapevine.

Our Julia | *Stephanie Barbé Hammer*

When I hear the name *Julia*, I think of the 1970's movie with Jane Fonda and Vanessa Redgrave about the mean lady playwright, whose name I have forgotten, who was Dashiell Hammett's mistress. My best friend from college loved that film and said I reminded her of the Julia character that Vanessa played.

It's strange how associations work, because I look nothing like Vanessa's Julia. And Yang Min, our translator at the Chongqing university where I am guest-teaching, tells me and my husband that her English name is also Julia – she looks like Vanessa even less.

Julia is barely 5 feet tall, and she weighs 100 pounds at most. She is friendly, polite and patient, and runs everywhere to get us water, take us to our next appointment, and translate what 7 or 8 people are saying to us simultaneously as well as our responses back to them.

There is a talent show at the Chongqing university and we are guests of honor. There are a lot of contests and competitions here. Students vie with each other in ways that remind me and my husband of the New England summer camps that we New York kids went to where everyone was desperately trying to be better and faster and more agile than everyone else so that we would be ready to fight the Communists if they landed in Manhattan or Long Island during the school year.

So it's a little bit funny that we are in this Communist country *now* and everyone is doing activities that feel like America in the early 60's.

We watch some singing and dancing and then a girl comes out on stage with nun chucks. She demonstrates a complex martial arts routine.

We applaud.

Then she lights the nun chucks on fire. And does the routine again. The flaming weapons dance in the air, twirling and twisting like
  red stars.

Who is that girl? says my husband.
That's our Julia, I tell him.

High Desert | *Shannon Phillips*

Sometimes when I'm trying to sleep,
I imagine the lap of an angel.
The light from wings buffers us from

anxiety, anguish,
freezes them into stillness,
like hovering matter
forming a planet,
waiting for the core
to start spinning again.

I don't know where this came from;
I'm not religious though I was baptized Catholic.
My grandmother taught me the rosary
and how to pray properly,
but it all stopped
when

my parents moved us to the desert
where property was cheap
and they could ride dirt bikes
and yell as loud as they wanted
when they fought.

On my walk to school,
I had to watch out for
rattlesnakes
and dogs that weren't fenced in.

SHORT STORIES FROM PAKISTAN

Zaibunnisa's *Mushaira*
Sana Munir

The grand hall in the Visitor's Palace was decked with ornaments of the most exquisite kind: a *gulpaash* carved out of jade, a chandelier fashioned with crystal upon which a hundred candles burnt bright and the centerpiece of the chandelier was another skillfully crafted sphere of glass with hexagonal inlets. Dried bark of the cinnamon, sandalwood and musk trees were put in the sphere so that the heat from the hundred candles aided to give out whiffs of a mixed spicy scent, that infused with the fragrance of those countless red and white roses which Princess Zaibunnisa had instructed to be placed on every inch of the floor not covered with silken Iranian carpets.

"Let them enjoy the flowers strewn under their feet," Zaibunnisa smiled as she spoke to Asha, her assistant while the latter helped her lady to dress up for the occasion.

Asha, stood behind Zaibunnisa and took her while to fix a garland of jasmine on the princess's lustrous and unbraided long locks. Zaibunnisa herself looked into the mirror, making sure the gold coin studded with grain-sized rubies and sapphires was in place: just the center of her forehead, right above the arch of her nose and the exact middle of her eye brows. "Shall I give you your veil, My Lady?"

"Ah, what for? I shall be behind sheaths of curtains, don't you know, my dear Asha?" Zaibunnisa twirled on her light feet as she turned to speak to her constant companion in the *zenankhana* – the Ladies' Chamber – in the fort of Lahore, the red brick castle built by her great grandfather, Emperor Akbar, with bastions and high walls that protected its entirety.

"Of course," Asha replied, embarrassed for sounding naïve.

"When my great grandfather introduced the *zenankhana* to the royal family, he made sure women stayed out of sight of all the men in the world, except for those related to them by marriage or blood-kin." Asha sat on the purple velveteen chair fashioned like a throne, just beside the mirror. Asha knew what to do so she quickly squatted on the floor, although her *choorridaar pajama* stung at the bend of her knees but that is what protocol demanded, to sit immediately below the level of the princess when she was seated on her chair. "And now, I, Zaibunnisa Makhfi, daughter of Aurangzeb Alamgir, have stepped out of these tall walls to speak with men, and topple them at their own game."

"You make up your verses with such class, my princess, I am always awed." Asha enjoyed these conversations with Zaibunnisa.

"You are sweet, Asha. I have to fight my father for this, but the books I have acquired, to fill that library next to my room, or the Kashmiri manuscript writers I have hired to copy books for me to distribute among men and women of Lahore, are not helping me curtail the desire I have in me to write," Zaibunnisa looked into the air, confessing her unease with the restrictions that bound her no matter how hard she tried.

Asha watched her lady's face, as if a child would look at the moon – awed and attentive, not knowing how to respond, but intensely locking eyes with the image before their eyes. "Let us get ready, Asha," the princess broke their trance.

"Which one shall it be, My Lady?" Asha unfastened the metal snap of the Kashmiri wooden box which held Zaibunnisa's gold, silver and pearly anklets.

"The gold one, whose tinkling bells can be heard from one end of the hall to the other," Zaibunnisa replied, fixing the loose strand of hair caught up in her *chaandbaali*, the huge hoop of gold she wore in her earlobes.

Asha smiled. "Ah, they already sigh, sick with admiration, at the sound of your voice, my princess, why make them more miserable with the tinkles?"

Zaibunnisa laughed aloud, something she only did when she was in the *zenankhana*. "They have come from afar and away, to meet one another, become royal guests for a week to enjoy my father's bounties. Why would you think they would pine for me, silly Asha?"

"Why, my lady, this slave knows your heart belongs to the handsome and knighted prince Sipihr, son of your favourite uncle, Dara Shikoh, and none of these poets have a chance of getting up close to you, but your mesmerizing poetry, in your titillating voice can bewitch anyone, my princess. I do not find them at fault."

Zaibunnisa set down her foot upon which Asha had already tied the tinkling anklet. It was a dozen chains of gold and upon each chain hung two dozen tiny spherical globes. "Has Uncle arrived yet?"

"I have not heard of it, but the trumpet shall be blown, no doubt, once His Highness enters, wouldn't it?"

"Certainly, the future king deserves all glory and respect." Zaibunnisa examined both her feet, the tops of whom had been decorated with a pattern of henna and the toes ornate with toe-rings. "The silken shoes shall do," she spoke softly, her mind wandering upon the moment to see her beloved Sipihr if he had chanced upon accompanying his father to their side of the fort. Nonetheless, she was looking forward to see her favourite uncle, Prince Dara Shikoh, the poet and the reader. The one who had taught her to love books and the written word, especially one written in verse.

"All done, my lady." Asha stood up, tucked away the jewelry box and folded her hands, a sign of waiting for the next command.

"Have the manuscript writers left, already?" she asked Asha.

The girl was confused. "I am sorry if I am wrong, princess, but did you not ask them to take leave on Friday, so they could only arrive as guests for the *mushaira*?"

"Oh yes, of course, I did, thank you, Asha." Zaibunnisa was slightly disappointed for the rare book of Persian poetry she had borrowed from her uncle was to be returned today, after her team of manuscript writers, stationed in the library or *maktabkhana* of her part of the palace had reproduced several copies of it, to be gifted to the poets who had arrived, upon her invitation from all corners of her grandfather Shah Jahan's empire in the subcontinent. Some had come from Persia, there were a couple from Constantinople, one from Arabia and another who was running late from China. They all wrote Persian verse, as did Zaibunnisa, but she had a grasp over Urdu, too. However, the language for the *mushaira* she had arranged, and did every year, was Persian. So she cleared her throat, put her aflutter heart to rest and rose.

"Let's go, Asha, it shall be rude to arrive later than the esteemed guests themselves." She strode, her silken scarf doused in rich Arabian perfume scented the air as she walked through the arched doorways that would take her and Asha, to the Visitor's Palace.

"Have you spoken with the Royal Kitchen, today?" Zaibunnisa was suddenly the hostess of the first kind of literary festival in the region, instead of being the carefree princess that she was supposed to be.

"Yes, my princess. The menu you designed is being followed strictly."

"Teas of various flavours, sweets and nuts shall flow aplenty during the poetic symposium, okay?" She reminded her dressing assistant who turned into a personal assistant as soon as her role required her to be.

"Don't worry, my princess, I shall serve these things myself, if the need may arise."

Zaibunnisa stopped, and turned to look at the loyal girl who froze in her tracks, careful not to take one step further until her lady walked ahead. Zaibunnisa placed her hand on Asha's cheek and said, lovingly, "What would I do without you, dear Asha?"

"Ah my lady." The girl blushed, shy and happy, "There are a million Ashas to replace me but where would I be without your kindness and your poetry?"

Zaibunnisa laughed, but stopped just in time, before anyone else could hear her cackles. "You shall be just fine, writing poetry better than I, Asha."

"You embarrass me, my lady." Asha was about to burst with pride.

"And why not? You should write, if you can offer critique to my words when I ask, you could certainly write something of your own."

"As you please, my princess." Asha touched her forehead with the tips of her fingers with a cupped hand, a sign of obedience and appreciation.

"Good. Now let us go in, and render these poets speechless with the magic of our words," Zaibunnisa half spoke to Asha and half to herself, as she entered the hall, where she would stand behind a heavy curtain and spin magic with her words, like she did always, and left the poets in awe and in admiration. She saw, from behind the layers of chiffon and silk curtains, the poets sitting in a circular fashion. She being the only woman at the *mushaira*, sat behind the curtain with Asha and a couple more attendants. The man right in front of her eyes, from Lukhnow, was puffing at a *hookah* flavoured with roses and filled with the most preciously picked tobacco leaves. The one next to him, from Kabul, broke a piece of *laddoo* and offered some to the one next to him. On their right was a Kashmiri poet, the one who had praised Zaibunnisa last year for her poetry, and requested her to show her face, and he had the audacity to say so, during the *mushaira*, in verse!

The princess had shown him his place, in verse, too. "He is back again!" she whispered to Asha.

"I will feed him opium so he goes to sleep before he gets to say something silly." Asha gritted her teeth.

The princess muffled her laughter. "No, we don't treat our guests like that."

"Of course, my princess, I apologise." Asha bent her neck to show submission.

"Ah, it is alright. You mean well." Zaibunnisa took a deep breath, ready to announce her presence. Asha opened a small casket, made with silver and studded with *feroza* – Zaibunnisa's favourite stone. Inside were smaller caskets, made of gold and copper, filled with tobacco, betel-nuts, aniseed, rock-sugar, desiccated coconut, candied rose petals, catechu paste, licorice and betel leaves.

"Add extra catechu and licorice, Asha, to keep my throat clear."

"Yes, my lady," Asha nodded.

The lady spoke, and before she did, she swished one foot to touch the other, so the bells tinkled as if to make a prelude to her speech, "*Salam*, gentlemen. It is your humble host, Zaibunnisa Makhfi, who speaks to you, and welcomes you all to this rather modest gathering where words and verse unify us. *Aadaab!*"

In Search of a Muse

Mahnoor Tahir

In the old parts of the city lived a woman more ancient than the crumbling walls surrounding her. Her skin curled all over, dry as peeling paint. There was a faint tremor in her gnarled fingers so that whatever she touched trembled to her rhythm. Most captivating, however, were her piercing eyes.

When she smiled, a complicated web weaved itself around the corners of her eyes as they turned soft as buttermilk. In moments of rage, her gaze became pitch dark and bottomless. Most often they remained a mysterious hazel – the stasis between moments of excitement, the prelude to something extraordinary. It was in moments like these that she was most unpredictable.

My presence before her was something of a coincidence. I was between jobs. I was feeling uninspired and was in need of some intellectual stimulation. It had been a stroke of luck that I had decided to visit the *dhabba* at the same time as the woman's regular clients. It had been nothing but chance that I had overheard them talking.

"She could see my past, present and future. It was extraordinary," one man was insisting, his hands flying in elaboration of his astonishment.

The other was only too eager to reaffirm his partner's statements. "She is a witch. A seer," he said, nodding with the too-serious air of someone well-versed in whatever the other person was saying.

"I was a little sceptical at first. I mean there are quacks running all over this forsaken country. Who would believe that someone was gifted in such times?"

"No one, I'd expect. But she is touched by divinity," the other corrected reverently.

I was jolted out of eavesdropping when the dusty waiter brought me an equally dusty glass of *chai*. As I blew over it with daintiness that was sorely out of place in my shabby locality, I contemplated checking out the aforementioned place. If nothing else, it could give me something to write about.

With the decision solidified, I drained my scalding tea and tossed a couple of grimy notes on the worn formica table top before standing up. The two men turned to me instinctively, their conversation momentarily suspended. "Where can I find this woman?"

For a brief moment their faces remained blank, eyes glazed with staring at something inconsequential to them. Then the moment passed and they gave me precise instructions as is customary among my fellow nationals. With smiles on both sides, I left my new friends to their bonding over *chai* and followed their instructions to the heart of the city.

There was something transcendent about old Lahore. Perhaps it was the way urbanism had tried to encroach upon nature but instead of total dominion, had achieved a kind of seamless harmony. Perhaps it was those ancient buildings, observing the passing time through their boxy windows. Almost sentient.

The address I was after was much deeper than I had ever been before. At the end of a narrow, twisting road surrounded by houses on all sides, it was nestled precariously between two others of its kind, their floors jutting uneasily outwards. I climbed the steps to the metal door, noticing the option of a bell and a lock-pull. I rang the bell, wondering who simply pulled that discreet divot and entered this strange house.

Less than seven minutes later, I was seated in my host's 'spirit room', admiring the crude artwork adorning the walls. The room was sparsely furnished and what little furniture there was, was in bright colours but woefully threadbare. A single *hookah* sat next to the circular table, emitting unconscious little puffs of pale, milky smoke.

The soft rustle of her beaded curtain was the only warning I received before the hunched woman came to settle before me. In that single second she gave me a multitude of shocking stimuli, fairly challenging my perceptions to keep up. Then she spoke. A single sentence. "What brings you to Begum Shehnai's esteemed house?" The words were delivered in a voice as smoky as her *hookah*.

I had never visited mediums before. I had a healthy amount of curiosity but I also possessed the keen edge of scepticism. I had decided long ago, using these two useful faculties, that seers and such were nothing but crooks. The Begum's eyes dared me to give voice to such thoughts, the gaze searing into my mind.

I cleared my throat awkwardly. "I don't know. Curiosity, maybe?" It was the truth but underneath her eagle eyes, it turned into a question and my voice squeaked in an undignified manner. She had a strangely powerful presence.

The Begum seemed unimpressed. Her gnarled fingers tapped a slow rhythm on the table top, sending a shiver skittering down my back. "I sense a loss in you. An emptiness. What is it you look for?"

The words of those two men came back to me. *She's a witch,* they'd said. My fingers knotted underneath the table and unbidden, the words were out. "I have lost my ability to write. I can't find my muse. It's like I can't find beauty or joy in anything around me. I wish to reconnect with my inspiration, the ones I looked up to." I sounded desperate. Painfully aware of how others in my position must have sounded exactly the same.

Her mouth quirked, finding my pleading amusing. "Who is your inspiration?"

I wasn't entirely unprepared for the question. I had wrestled with it all my life. People around me had judged me for my choice and I had persisted almost rigidly in admiring the same people, partly to thumb my nose at our carefully contained culture. "Some foreign writers," I began, naming a few haltingly.

She pursed her lips. I wasn't sure she knew, let alone understood, the implications of such literary legends. "I suppose they would fit right in over here." She was mocking me but there was nothing humorous in her countenance. She flipped her hands which had been laying palms down this entire time. In them she held a dried shrub. "It's time for Begum Shehnai to help you find what you've lost."

Unceremoniously, she dumped the dried stalks in front of me and closed her eyes. Within seconds the room was filled with hoarse humming, mingling with the smoke of the *hookah* and the smell of *agarbati* in the room. I felt my head getting woozy, my senses light. When I wobbled in my chair, I reached instinctively to grab the table. In doing so, I touched the dried shrub.

The world shifted instantly. It became a place of shadows and smoke. I saw groups of men walking by me, women in the marketplace by the dozen. The heady feeling was still there but slowly the shadows gained substance, colour rushed everywhere. I stumbled forward. The merchants called out to attract customers and I saw an array of colourful shawls and pottery and antiques.

A kid in *kurta shalwar* ran towards me, standing a few feet away, and called out. "The King's procession will pass by in a few minutes." Then he was skipping away. Instinctively, I followed.

Through the overflowing marketplace, the narrow alleys, the rushing carts and bicycles, I passed with a sense of wonder. Then the kid stopped, leaning against a shimmering building with small, box-like windows. Across the street, two elephants came trundling by. Their backs carried large *palkies,* and I could just make out the King's jewelled turban.

I registered the crowd around me. A man nearby looked at the approaching procession and called out a flattering verse to the King. A pouch of gold was thrown at his feet for his delicacy with words. I expected him to grapple over the gold. It was what the norm was for us. What we had become. But what I got were men springing up to shout more verses. A battle of skill. They all wanted to be heard. Wanted to compete. A writer's curse. But here, there were people who actually listened, who wanted to. The crowd was cheering them on, oblivious that the procession had passed.

I broke away from the crowd, feeling distinctly detached. It had never occurred to me to look up the period of literary genius in my own national history. The literary giants I admired had always suffered and mourned and slogged through their writing. And yet, a man in a street was capable of such poetic beauty in the spur of a moment. I felt as if to peek inside his mind would be a wondrous experience.

It all felt like a lie. The strange Urdu verses were still ringing in my ears. Haunting, lonely, joyous, and celebratory. They contained a wealth of emotion. The depth I had been lacking. I tried to remember the last time I had written something that had tugged my own heart. I could not.

The dream scene had changed while I was lost in contemplation. When I registered it, I was surrounded by shadows once again but instead of forming into clear figures, they remained aloof, wisps of smoke circling me. From the depths came thunderous voices. Wounded and angry.

"We were no saints, but we had feelings. Strong feelings for this nation, its uprising."

"We were the voices that guided a revolution."

"We were the pivots that turned a King's court. That dictated the sequence of history."

"We were a dime a dozen – a nation of poets – but essential. Lauded and respected."

"Our words were cherished, revered. We sat and ate with the King himself."

"We were the very pinnacle of success. We could turn away anyone we wanted."

As the voices got louder, I put my hands to my ears and forced myself to relax. My heart hammered against my chest. I felt like fainting. Just as my vision began to turn black, a single couplet rang clear as day in my aching head.

"Thy abode is not on the dome of a royal palace; You are an eagle and should live on the rocks of mountains."

The words from a forgotten Urdu lesson rang in my head as I slammed back to reality. My hands shook and I had to press them against my thighs to keep them steady. Across from me, Begum Shehnai was observing me with shrewd eyes, her mouth once again crooked in amusement.

"What you were missing was never your muse," she said cryptically, folding her hands demurely over the dried herb once again.

I paid her and left, my footsteps loud and quick. I felt jittery as if everything inside me had been picked apart and rearranged. She knew somehow. She had done something. I came here to find inspiration but had found something else entirely.

When later that day, I read the poem my saving verse had come from, I smiled. In the depths of my roots, I had found what the Begum had known all along I needed. In that jolting glimpse of the past, I had found my purpose, my muse!

The Incident
Taha Kehar

Apa Saeeda ironed my sequin-embellished dress for the dinner party and laid it out on my bed. Raising her frail fingers against her forehead in a polite *adaab*, our old retainer smiled at me and blinked back tears of unbridled joy. Intuitively, I jumped up from the rocking chair next to the window, dashed towards her and slung my arms around her shoulders. With my head resting against her neck and her hands gently patting my back, I felt the familiar warmth of her body. With each passing second, it seemed as if my mind had been lulled into a state of calm, relieved of its usual dilemmas.

"Where have you been, *Apa* Saeeda?" I asked her as she sat next to me on my bed. "I came looking for you in the kitchen. I also checked the servant quarters. There was no sign of you. Where were you?"

"I'd gone to the supermarket to buy a few things," she said. "I'm making your favourite dishes for tonight's *dawat* – *biryani*, *korma*, *saag*, you name it! But first tell me, how does it feel to be back home?"

Her question exerted a magnetic field, drawing other concerns and memories into it. In the six hours since my plane had landed on the tarmac at Jinnah International Airport, no one – not even my parents – had asked me how it felt to return to the city of my childhood mutinies, the Karachi that I had surrendered without my volition. Before I boarded the flight from London and decided to break away from my settled life in that alien metropolis, I had made a conscious attempt to stay abreast of the news from Karachi. I knew that the MQM had steadily lost ground and that the city's violent past had become just that – a dark chapter of its history which people were struggling to forget. Since Karachi's raging storms had passed, I didn't understand why I had to seek refuge in my adoptive city anymore.

"I want to come back," I'd told *Amma* over the phone. "It's been so many years. It's time for me to come back to my roots. Besides, I'm sick of meeting you and *Baba* during your trips to London. I want to see you in our house. I want to eat dinner in our dining room, watch TV in our living room and sleep in my own room."

Stunned into silence, *Amma* listened quietly to my nostalgic musings about our Karachi home. Throughout my years at boarding school, my mother had been a distant yet well-meaning visitor. After many years of treading the path she had chalked out for me, I'd summoned the strength to deviate from her plan, to pursue a selfish instinct.

"*Beti*, don't be silly," she'd finally said. "You have a great job in London. So many people would kill to have such an enviable legal career. And you want to throw it all away for an idea of home?"

Though I had eventually disregarded her concerns, *Amma* was right. I was throwing away the life I had cultivated in that cold little island I now called home. Not for an idea of home but for a flavour of it, a whiff of the childhood that I'd left behind. In the long years that I'd spent away from Karachi, my mind had been teeming with the games Zara – *Apa* Saeeda's daughter, who was six years older than me – and I played in the garden of our home in Muslimabad. Zara would always win at *baraf pani* and *pakram pakrai* because she had stamina and could run a marathon with all the energy she'd stored up. I remember the time when she'd dashed through the track at the Gymkhana playground and I had to accept my defeat.

"*Apa* Saeeda," I said as curiosity jolted me out of my reverie. "Where is Zara? Is she going to come see me soon?"

The old retainer's smile disappeared and a ghostly pallor took its place. She lowered her head and turned away from me, as if she were hiding a secret from me. Her silence puzzled me, making me wonder if I'd said something to offend or upset her.

"What's the matter?" I demanded, distressed by her strange reaction. "Where's Zara?"

"*Apa* Saeeda," a sullen voice rose from the entrance of my room. I craned my neck and saw *Amma* standing with her hand clasped against the wooden door. *Apa* Saeeda got up from the bed with a jerk and dutifully nodded as her employer waddled into the room.

"Run into the kitchen and ensure that the cutlery is squeaky clean," *Amma* said in a low voice that made her instructions sound like a request instead of an order. "I don't want Alizeh to think I'm a negligent *begum sahib* with incompetent servants."

Apa Saeeda smiled wanly to just about acknowledge the fact that *Amma* had made a joke that wasn't particularly funny and then scurried back into the kitchen.

"Go get ready, Laila," *Amma* said, gently tapping my shoulder. "The guests will be arriving soon. I don't want them to think..."

"*Amma*," I interrupted her. "Where's Zara?"

"Who's that?" my mother responded impassively.

"*Apa* Saeeda's daughter," I said. "Surely you remember her? She was in the car with us when we went to Aunty Alizeh's wedding – the day before I left for boarding school in London."

"Laila," *Amma* snapped. "Don't dwell on the past. Now that you've decided to come back to this godforsaken city, you'll have to erase the memory of that incident if you want to survive."

But I couldn't erase the memory of the incident that had compelled my parents to send me to boarding school, away from my idyllic childhood. As *Amma* left the room, I was tempted to confide in her about the night when we were mugged after returning from Aunty Alizeh's wedding. I wanted to remind my mother of how she had frantically instructed me to slide down the back seat of our Corolla and lie flat on the dusty mat without making a sound. I wanted to tell her that I'd followed her orders and placed a finger on my lips while she, *Apa* Saeeda and Zara draped a black *dupatta* over me.

I don't remember what happened next. As a six-year-old, I didn't perceive the dangers of a holdup and allowed the enveloping darkness to draw me into deep slumber. The next morning, I woke up in my own bed. A few hours later, we boarded a flight to London. Zara and *Apa* Saeeda weren't there to see us off at the airport.

"I'm glad you decided to come back home," Aunty Alizeh said, her voice muffled by the spoonful of *biryani* she'd put into her mouth.

"Your mother missed you dearly."

My parents smiled at their guests, momentarily forgetting their initial apprehensions about my decision to move back to Karachi.

Uncle Jamil, her husband, gulped down a glass of chilled water and cleared his throat.

"I agree, Laila," he said as he placed the glass on a coaster. "Honestly, it was a terrible idea to send you away after the mugging. It's not like the city had become unlivable. Everyone thought there were criminals and self-styled militants roaming the streets. But all of us stayed back and we're still alive."

"Exactly," I exclaimed. "I doubt anyone left London after the 7/7 bombings or the recent shootouts."

Baba cast a grim look in my direction. I lowered my gaze and twirled my fork around in a plate, unsure if my defiance had upset him.

"Jamil, we were just trying to do what was best for our daughter," *Baba* said defensively, with a scowl painted on his wrinkled face.

"Sabir Bhai," Uncle Jamil piped up. "There's a trick to living in a city like Karachi. If you escape a mugging attempt unharmed, you're lucky. But I also believe that escaping gives you the skills you need to survive. Our Laila was lucky and probably has the survival instinct in her. Unlike *Apa* Saeeda's daughter who was..."

Baba nudged Uncle Jamil and clicked his tongue in disapproval. I flung my fork against my plate and stared inquiringly at my parents, livid that they had kept this secret from me for all these years.

"Are you talking about Zara?" I questioned Uncle Jamil. "What happened to her? Why was she unlucky?"

Alarmed by my curiosity, *Amma* rose from her armless chair and served her guests another helping of *biryani* and *korma*.

"Why aren't all of you eating?" she chimed nervously. "This is a celebration. My daughter has come back."

Ignoring her attempts to change the subject, I shot a disapproving frown at Uncle Jamil, hoping that he wouldn't disappoint me by withholding the truth. *Baba* heaved an exasperated sigh, as if he'd made a mistake.

"I'm sorry," Uncle Jamil said after a pregnant pause. "I thought you knew. How would you have known, anyway? You slept through the entire incident. Your mother did the right thing by making sure you were hiding in the backseat. It was late at night so the muggers couldn't have spotted you. Anyway, they robbed your mother's jewellery and cash. They even took *Apa* Saeeda's fake gold set. But she wasn't worried about that. After all, they gunned down her daughter."

"Zara is dead?" I blurted, turning towards my parents. "And you didn't bother to tell me that. Why did you keep this a secret?"

"You were so young," Amma said, affectionately placing her arms around me. "You were so close to Zara and we wanted to protect you from the pain. We sent you away because it seemed easier than raising you in this insecure city. We also stopped *Apa* Saeeda from telling you."

"But she could have run," I wailed. "She ran so fast."

A mix of anger and guilt coursed through my veins. Overwhelmed with grief, I realised that my recollections about that night were fragmented and self-indulgent, nothing compared with Zara's fate or *Apa* Saeeda's loss. Yet, I was the one who had gained the opportunity to escape the sound of the gunshots that killed Zara and her memory that had lived longer than she had. *Apa* Saeeda had stayed on in the city where her daughter had died, silently enduring the pain of her absence.

With a long sigh, I ran into the kitchen. *Apa* Saeeda was holding a bowlful of *halwa* in a tray crammed with small bowls and spoons. When she caught sight of my tear-stricken face, the old retainer placed the tray on the counter.

"What happened, *beti*?" she asked, baffled to see a grown woman sob like a child.

"Zara," I yelled, my voice choked with emotion. "Zara!"

Apa Saeeda exhaled deeply as she held me in a warm embrace, tears rolling down her face and moistening her cheeks.

"It's okay," she reassured me.

A gloomy silence pervaded the room for the few minutes that I mourned a childhood loss as an adult.

"I'm glad you're back home," *Apa* Saeeda asked, breaking the stillness with her cheerful voice. "It feels like my own daughter has come home."

In My Land Lie Embedded My Roots
I Have Nurtured Them With My Blood
Zakia Nasir

The beautifully decorated hall was all lit up. It literally dazzled my eyes. I had gone to a family friend's daughter's wedding. A stranger to this army gathering and to Islamabad elite, I paused in the entrance to see if I could find a familiar face. Glittering army wives had their own circles. I took a few steps forward casting a cursory glance around for a possibility to find a seat in the huge gathering. I am not shy but reticent of talking to total strangers. My eyes alighted on a soberly dressed dignified looking lady with a sad smile on her lips and the sadness reaching her beautiful hazel eyes. I couldn't guess why she passed me a smile. Maybe we exchanged sympathetic vibes. Finding some chairs vacant on her table, as she seemed to have taken up an aloof seat, I crossed the hall and sat near her. After the formal greetings I exchanged some pleasantries with her before fully introducing myself and trying to get to know her.

She was a nice decent lady who told me about her husband who was a retired army officer. I asked her about her children. She was quiet for a while. Then she told me she had two sons and a daughter. There was something in her tone that really intrigued me. I kept quiet for some time, and then just to keep the conversation going I asked her where she lived and told her I had come from Lahore and was a professor. She smiled. Yes at one of their postings she also taught in a college she told me. She recalled how she used to walk her children to school. The younger one went crying to the playgroup, as he wanted to stay home.

Moving on with our conversation, I enquired what the younger one did now. She had already told me the eldest was in the army and the daughter was studying medicine.

She was quiet for a long time. Her eyes filled with tears. She sat still trying to control the silent sobs that seemed to choke her from within. With a great effort she rose out of the silent grief. I was silent too. Overwhelmed and awed I did not know what to say. Sympathetic tears welled up in my eyes. They always do whenever I see anybody crying. I hugged her because I felt like doing it, wanted to share the grief, which was still not known to me.

"He was very handsome. Too intelligent for his age." She spoke while wiping her tears. "Twice he got double promotions. When he passed his FSC he wanted to join the army. He had a passion to fight for his country. He had a desire to sacrifice his life for Pakistan and be a *Shaheed*. We already had a son in the army. We wanted him to study abroad. He said his roots were here. He belonged to this soil; he would not give up his passion. The three years when he studied abroad, we found out afterwards that on each page of his notebook everyday he wrote *Shaheed* Capt. Usman. The first thing he did after completing his engineering abroad, he registered for recruitment in the army."

"How could we stop him?" she continued. "We as an army family had vowed to sacrifice our lives for our homeland. I never even knew about it. It was only when he received the selection letter. Face red with jubilation he showed it to us. I kissed his forehead and hugged my lovely son to my heart."

"We sent him with blessings and prayers. I remember how he always said, *Mama, I am the son of this soil. My roots belong here. Pray I become a martyr. It is my desire that I shed my blood on this soil. Don't be sad. More sons from this soil will rise and be ready to protect the land.*" She took a deep breath, "True we belong here! Our roots are embedded in this land. But how can a mother let her handsome young accomplished son to go away just like that?"

The food had been served and there was a commotion around us. There was no desire in me to have food. But being coerced time and again we went towards the buffet. We returned with little on our plates and sat again. I didn't know how to begin the topic again. I didn't want to cause further pain, but I really was keen to know what happened.

She herself began, "Usman got a sword of honour. If you come to visit me, you would see that we have dedicated a room in our house to his accomplishments. His photo receiving the sword of honour and countless other memories adorn the walls." I promised I would visit her whenever I came to Islamabad in future. There was an uneasy silence as both of us concentrated on the food that tasted like saw dust. Then she began, "You know it's strange how I feel a certain affinity with you. We've never met! But it seems as if you are an old friend. When I saw you standing at the entrance looking around, there was a strange familiarity I sensed for you." I was overwhelmed. I could empathies with her, felt for her, cried for her but I was wordless.

She said, "After his training very soon he was promoted as he had an engineering degree from abroad. Then he was sent to Waziristan. Day and night I prayed for him. He wrote short notes always ending with the request to pray for his *shahadat*. How could I? I was his mother. I gave birth to him. He was a part of me. Once he came for a week's holiday. I pressured him to get engaged. He refused but couldn't really take the family pressure. He looked so handsome I could have given my life for him. That was the best week of my life. He was at home. Near us. Close to us, laughing joking having fun, making the whole house lit up by his joyous presence. When he was leaving I couldn't contain my tears. His sister hugged him tightly asking him to call frequently. His father stood strong and brave when we sent him off to

Waziristan again. Everyday there was news of officers and *jawans* being martyred. The Taliban were cruel, unscrupulous and brutal. Often he wrote to say how he was defending the land. They were difficult times. The sons of the soil were braving the brutal Taliban by sacrificing their lives. We were upset, anxious and worried. My husband always gave me emotional support. Two of our sons were fighting. One was fighting the external enemy and Usman, the enemy from inside. We had to pretend brave, stand upright, though a mother's heart shatters each time she hears of the martyrdom of the sons of the soil. We believe our roots are in this soil. We are the guardians of this land. We are proud our sons protect this land." Here she broke down. I wiped her tears. Tried to turn her chair away from seeing eyes. Stood in front of her uttering soothing words. In my heart for a moment I wished I had not met her. I was crying myself, my heart swollen with pain, but I couldn't make a show of it.

"Please *baji* control yourself; you are such a brave lady." She said she was. But not now. "One morning I was working in the kitchen and my daughter was watching the news. Another Capt. had been martyred along with four *jawans* while in an ambush against the Taliban in Waziristan. My daughter came to me anxiously, sadly telling me the news. I felt sad, again more mothers had lost their sons. What we didn't know at that time was that it was my Usman, my brave son who had stood bravely against the enemy and had borne the bullets on his chest, and doing so had killed many Taliban with his hand grenade."

"Half an hour later we had a phone call. A very officious sounding officer asked to talk to some male in the house. I felt faint and told him my husband was out. I was reeling with a blackout when my elder son called. From far off I could hear him say in the phone, *mama Mubarak ho, you are the mother of a Shaheed. Usman has sacrificed his life for his country. He has strengthened the roots of the land*, and he broke into sobs."

"I don't know when I gained consciousness. There was the coffin with the flag wrapped around it. I could not see my son's face. I could just see the coffin brought officially to our house. I received a diary written by him with the coffin. He was laid to rest with official protocol and respects. If you could say, it was a solace to be comforted by top army officials. Condolences were many. Sometimes people came and sat mum, such was the grief. I myself was quiet most of the time."

Then she began, "His friends came, those who were with him at the time of *shahadat*. They told how he bore the bullets on his chest but did not turn back, hurling the hand grenade he held in his hand towards the enemy killing many."

"After a few days I opened the diary. The first page read *Shaheed* Capt. Usman. I could read no further. After a few days again I approached the diary. It said, *mother please forgive me for wanting martyrdom, I should stay alive and serve you, but in my heart there is a passion to die for my land. I want the status of a Shaheed. Be happy I will take you to jannah with me.* I cried and cried. I am a *Shaheed's* mother I shouldn't cry I said to myself. But I can't help it. I turned the next page. *Please mother request my fiancée to forgive me too. I did not want to inflict any pain on her.* And thus almost every day's chronicles had one wish on top of the page, the desire for *Shahadat*. The son of the soil gave his blood to keep the roots green."

14 Days
Aaisha Umt Ur Rashid

"What on earth have you done for me all these years?" I stormed
at her. "Nothing, right? So why should I even cater your
excuses?" I was mad with rage, the rage that I had no power to
control. "I have come home after so many days and you have no
compassion for my needs. I wish *Abba* was alive."

Her wrinkled features became craggier with the grossness of
my voice. The fear in her gloomy eyes doubled when the tone of
my voice turned into shrieks. But it wasn't my fault as I
desperately needed money and like always, she didn't have any.
Slowly getting up from the ragged brunette couch, she leaned
towards me. Her sleek trembling fingers touched my shoulder
and her parched lips struggled with words. "I promise I will
arrange for it by tomorrow," the shaky voice assured me.

"Leave me alone, will you?" I shook her feeble hand away
mercilessly which felt like a hot coal. "And if you can't since you
are always feigning sickness, I think I better leave." My irritation
grew further.

"And yes, if you think I would come back this time, you are
wrong, *Ma*."

Furious over my life and fate, I sprang up from my place and
rushed towards the main door. She didn't have the energy to run
after me but her skinny arm stretched and her rickety lips
mumbled my name. Drenched in the ferocity of my anger, I
ignored that and left.

After *Abba's* death, *Ma* and I moved into a small one-room cottage in *Charrar pind*. This was done as a favor by the owner of the place who knew *Abba* when he was an accountant at a law firm situated in Defence where he had his case filed. Whatever little help *Abba* could afford, he did it. The owner felt really obliged for that and returned the favor much later to his grieved widow by providing this shelter. The rent was nominal, the place was enough for the two of us, but the irony was, this *pind* was situated right in the heart of Defence, which was considered the biggest hub of riches and wealth in the city, and I was fond of luxuries. Luxuries that *Ma* could not afford for me. I didn't even know how she was managing my college fee. But I didn't care much about that anyway. All my friends belonged to poor class families and when I sometimes passed by the gate separating my wretched village from its posh neighbour in my old cotton pants and *Abba's* worn-out shirt, the people always seemed to be mocking me. I could always hear their laughter and this doubled my desire to be like them, to be envied rather than being a source of amusement. I didn't want this poor life. I wanted to own luxuries and become a rich man.

Soon after we shifted here, having nothing else to do after college, I made friends with some of the bandits of my village. This made my interest in studies vanish and I started missing classes. I even stopped going home for days and weeks as one of these boys owned a *dhabba* where we all could stay, smoke cigarettes and plan our unknown future. *Ma* never objected to that. I never let her. She always feared making me angry and I always took advantage of being her only son.

Very soon, having discovered a spark in me to do the impossible for the fulfillment of my dreams, my friends introduced me to a business that could link me to the spoiled brats of rich businessmen in Defence. It was not long before I was a much wanted name amongst them. From my secret source, I brought to them what they wanted, all varieties. Opium, Hashish and even Marijuana. I sometimes even felt tempted to try one of these myself, but some internal instinct forbade me and I stuck only to delivery rather than consumption of it.

Now that the world was facing this God-dammed pandemic, my business was going down. There were rumors of people catching the disease and dying of it. Public places and markets were being closed. The local merchants almost ceased all trade due to the fear of being exposed to this virus. The gate linking the *pind* to Defence was locked down with heavy security. Though there was little awareness and understanding of this whole affair in the *pind*, I could sense the terror peeping through people's eyes. The streets were less crowded in the evenings now. Children were not seen playing outside the houses. Even the birds stopped chirping in the trees. It seemed as if everything was in a state of crisis. But I didn't care much about that either. All I could think of was money and ways to find it. I had used all my savings and now the payments had to be done in advance to buy drugs as the dealers no longer trusted me for post-delivery disbursements. Tonight I had promised the dealer to pick up my order but my pockets were empty and like always, *Ma* spoiled the whole plan.

Rushing a couple of streets away from my house cursing my existence, I grabbed my phone and rang up the dealer.

"Can I pick the stuff up and pay you later?" I whispered reaching the corner of the street.

"Get lost, you mugger, you already owe me ten thousand rupees."

Desperate in anger, I smashed my phone against the closed shutter of a shop. It made a shrill sound amidst the creepy silence of the street. But no one saw me do that. Taking a deep breath and mustering up some courage, I collected and reassembled the pieces. The screen wasn't working. I shook it a couple of times holding back my resentment. Just then I heard a meager ring tone but since the display screen was broken, I couldn't see who it was. I guessed where the accept button was and pressed it.

"Where the hell do you think you are?" It was Rana's voice. My throat felt dry.

"You were supposed to deliver my order three days back. I came searching for you and saw an ambulance at your door. They were taking your mother to the hospital, the neighbors told me. Is she suffering from Covid-19? If yes then please cancel all deliveries. I will let the group know about it and I am sure you would have to cancel all of their orders too."

My head swirled. *Ma?*

The next moment I found myself running. Running in the streets to find home. "Where the hell did it go? Which street was it in?" In this bewilderment my senses weren't working properly. Turning the corner of a street, I saw Aunty Shakeela and realized I was near home as her house was next to mine. There was no sign of any ambulance in the street. No sirens. No stretchers. I kicked the door open and hurled in the house. *Ma* was nowhere. My heart started sinking. Just then I heard a knock on the opened door. It was Aunty Shakeela.

"Where were you, boy?" She avoided coming in.

"I... I..." My mind turned blank.

"She was feeling terrible since last week so I told her to stay home and not go to work," Aunty Shakeela disclosed.

"Work?" I muttered.

"Yes, work. She does the washing in four houses in Defence. But why would you care, you hardly come home. She is always distressed because of you, boy, always guilty that she couldn't provide you a comfortable life," she sighed. "Anyways, I introduced her to these *bajis* a few months back. I also go with her and do the ironing. But she had high fever since last week, so

I was advised to tell her to stay home. They even got her blood tests done. But why am I even telling you all this? I seriously doubt sometimes that you are her real son. She is suspected of having Covid-19. But they are not sure. Some more tests and chest x-rays are needed. I wonder what will they do to her. I've heard they don't even let your family meet you for 14 days when you get this virus."

"14 days?" The number floated in front of my eyes.

She was saying things beyond my meager understanding. How could this be that she had been this sick and I didn't even notice? I did come home last week, to ask for money, I remembered. And even today. Her pale face appeared in front of my eyes. "Oh God." I took my head in my hands and sat on the floor. "Her hand was burning when I shook it away," I remembered. "Have I been this ignorant of her plight?" My senses were turning numb and my vision was slowly getting blurred.

The next morning, when I woke up, I was on the floor near the couch. Didn't know when I fell asleep last night. My whole body was aching and my muscles felt stretched. I looked around the room. For the first time in all these years I was examining this small house. In one corner, there rested a small wooden table with a broken leg. On the table laid a hand-stitched *kamiz* neatly ironed and folded. I couldn't even remember it was mine. Next to the table was a *charpai* on which I slept whenever I came home. *Ma* always chose to sleep on the floor near the *charpai* saying she felt comfortable there. I never minded that. Besides, how often did I come home?

I felt hungry so I looked around for something to eat. I remembered I left home in anger without eating the food that *Ma* had made for me. I searched for that. Covered under a *chaabi*, I found a small tray having *daal chawal* in a plate. Famished as I was, I finished the rice in no time and drank the glass of water that was kept with the tray. My thirst wasn't quenched so I got up to refill my glass from the water cooler. It was empty.

Just then the door knocked.

It was Aunty Shakeela again. She was carrying a tray having two *chappatis* and some gravy in a bowl. "You must be hungry," she handed over the tray to me angrily. "And here is a bottle of water. Your *Ma* borrowed some water from me yesterday for you which I am sure must be finished by now."

The nerves of my brain felt like twitching.

"And here is the money." She thrust an envelope in my hand.

"Money…?" I couldn't understand what was going on.

"Yes, money that you need. When you left home yesterday, your *Ma* asked me to arrange for some money for an urgent need that had befallen you," she said sarcastically. "I asked two of the *bajis* and they gave me this money today as advance salary of your *Ma* for two months."

My body was drenched in sweat. I couldn't utter a word.

"I am sure your dire need would be fulfilled with this money and she would be at ease in the hospital." Aunty Shakeela wiped her tears with the corner of her *dupatta*. "And if she cannot fight the virus and get back home recovered, I will work in her place for two months."

Something shook inside of me, like an electric current. "Fight the virus? *Ma* has got that deadly virus that the world is so damn scared of? And what if it takes her life?" My eyes suddenly felt misty.

"By the way," Aunty Shakeela continued, "What keeps you at home? When she was here, I hardly saw you in this house, she was always waiting for you, all alone. Don't you have your important chores outside anymore? Were you only waiting for her to leave so that you could stay here independently?" She banged the door and left.

The words felt like hammer smacks on my mind. "Isn't that true?" I crumpled the envelope in my hand in rage, the rage that I had no power to control. "Isn't that awfully true that I have been a very bad son to my *Ma*?" The mist in my eyes turned into droplets and started dripping out. "Oh *Ma*..." I whispered, "Please come back so that I can be the good son that you always wanted me to be."

Wiping the tears with the back of my hands, I placed the envelope on the table and moved around the room. I could feel her presence around me, her fragrance was there in everything I touched. Her shawl, her clothes, her comb, everything had that same aura that the persona had herself. "Damn the virus." I picked her shawl up and wrapped it around my shoulders. It felt so soothing. As if I had just hugged her.

The next morning I got up with a knock on the door. "Must be Aunty Shakeela," I thought and opened the door. It was a young man with a mask on his face and a box in his gloved hands.

"Yes?" I inquired.

"Mrs. Iqbal has sent this for you." The man informed me.

"But I don't know anyone with this name." I felt puzzled.

"Your mother does," the man handed over the box to me. "She works in her house. These are some edibles and things you might need during Ramadan. I also went to the hospital to see your mother. She is improving. But they will keep her for another 12 days or so. And she told me to strictly forbid you to visit her as she has not disclosed to the doctors that she has a son lest they may take you away too. She says you are her only reason to live. I am sure you know it is safer at home and you should not go outside unnecessarily. She also requested me to ask you if you need anything."

"*Ma*," my voice trembled. "I need my *Ma*."

"Pardon?" The man raised his brow.

"Nothing, Sir," I blinked my eyes to hide my tears. "Please thank Mrs. Iqbal for all this."

The box felt quite heavy. I placed it on the floor and opened it. It was full of supplies I considered luxuries. Milk, dates, juices, soft drinks. I kept looking at the things for a while. Did I need them? Did I need all these things and that money that Aunty Shakeela gave me yesterday? I picked up the envelope from the table and counted the money. It was enough to get all deliveries done. But the young man's words echoed in my ears... *She says you are her only reason to live.*" A shiver ran down my spine. "And what have I done in return for her? Instead of serving her in this old age, I have always been a nuisance. Oh, how she used to get scared when I stormed at her for my needs... how I always yelled and shrieked at her... and her eyes? ...that fear in her eyes... those parched lips trying to whisper my name... the trembling wrinkled hands... God... what have I been doing to the person who deserved the best of my behavior... Oh God... what have I done?"

It seemed as if the inside of my head was slowly opening. The emptiness of the small house was doing something magical to my senses. It was filling me up. The moment of epiphany was near... I could make amends. I could undo it all. I knew exactly what to do.

For the next few days, it was *Ma's Jai Namaz* and me. It had become my best friend as I started praying regularly. Every artery of my body, every thread of my soul and every scrap of my being had turned into a prayer. All my desires of owning the wealth and riches of this world had turned into a single longing... to get *Ma* back home. Every time I sat on the prayer mat, the flood of tears washed away all the layers of worldly wishes from my eyes making my vision clearer. I felt I was being cleansed by some divine force of all the immensity of sins that were attached to my soul. The sins that I had no power to shed myself. Now I knew that I would give a damn to the riches of the world just to get *Ma* back.

During one of these mornings, I was sitting on the prayer mat, making my recently developed connection with God stronger when I suddenly realized that, none of my friends that I trusted so much had contacted me in all these days. No phone calls. Not even once. This was enough to make things clear to my crowded brain. There was only one person on earth who cared for me and now I had decided to do for that person what she had been doing for me, even more. Yes, I decided to leave bad company and complete my degree, apply for a good, respectable job somewhere and earn good money to serve *Ma*. I wouldn't let her work in this old age. Lost in my thoughts, I didn't know when I slept on the prayer mat.

"Get up my son," *Ma's* soothing voice echoed in my ears.

In a frenzy... I got up and looked around. There was no one. My heart pumped fast. Just then there was a knock on the door.

I jumped up from my place and dashed to the door. It was her.

I froze. Was I looking at heaven itself? Was it a dream? I wanted to hug her tight and tell her how I had missed her all these days. But my body refused to synchronize with my wish. I wanted to hold her heavenly hands and kiss them... I wanted to tell her that I had changed... that I had realized my mistakes... but where to find that courage?

"*Ma*," was the only trembling word my tongue could utter.

"My son," she entered the house and took me in her arms. It was heaven. Yes. Or even more. She looked better and healthier. Mrs. Iqbal's driver had dropped her home. I made her sit comfortably on the couch, fetched a glass of water for her and sat on the floor near her. She looked surprised.

Deep in my mind, I was contemplating how some days teach you lessons nothing else can teach, some deprivations fill your empty love tanks to the core and some absences, even short ones, teach you the importance of presence. There are years that take away your sanity from you and there are days that lend it back. Today when I looked at *Ma's* face, which I hardly ever had time to do so before, I felt I was being blessed with the supreme bounties of the universe.

I looked at her wrinkled visage and kept looking. My retinas had encompassed a vision that was penetrating in my whole existence, easing out my soul. Unconsciously placing my hands on her feet, I burst into tears. Tears that I had no power to control. The flood of emotions that I had long concealed under the burden of my worldly desires had suddenly made a comeback. I felt as if I had woken up from a dream of oblivion. Her quarantine time had taught me lessons I wouldn't ever wish to unlearn. The mist was clearing up. I could see the light in her eyes, I could feel the warmth in her touch and now I knew that I was the richest man on earth as I had the most priceless blessing of God in front of me, my *Ma!*

Poisoned Roots

Areej Tahir

The room was dark, and there was a stench that made it uncomfortable to breathe. The bulb on my head kept flickering and amplified the lurking ominous feeling. I observed the moths drunk on love burning their wings every time they touched the bulb, yet never stopping and sweltering themselves until their wings gave out. The glass pane showed me my miserable reflection. Hair disheveled, eyes sunken and wrists raw from being handcuffed to the table. Her face flashed before me, and I remembered her eyes, looking just as hollow, just as void.

The door opened in a swift motion, and a man in a creased suit stepped in. He started introducing himself but every word he said was a gibberish whisper my mind failed to register. The silence of my thoughts was too loud.

"I need you to tell me what happened so I can help you."

Help.

The very word woke me up. It was my lawyer for the defense. How could he help me? I didn't need help anymore. There was nothing to live for. Or was there?

"I needed some money, so I went out to rob anyone I could," I said, my voice sounding foreign. And I wondered what she would have sounded like if she had said something.

There was silence, an actual one.

"What did you need money for?"

"My wife's cesarean section," I said as memories started flooding me. The memories that seemed to be images from an eccentric dream, with emotions overwhelming my mind. It was like a dream where the scene changes hastily, half of the sounds blur in the background, and you are left drenched in a cold sweat, indecisive and confused. I remember her screams, her gush of unexpected bleeding, the rapidly slowing heartbeat on the monitor and the doctor telling me I may lose all three of them. My wife never told me there were going to be twins. This was her 'surprise from heaven'.

"I had lost my job two weeks ago, and my health-card by the company was nullified. I did not have enough saved for the normal delivery, let alone a C section," I told him, unintentionally but painfully scoffing. I wondered if thoughts this loud could be heard by the others.

I called my friends, my family, and my colleagues, but everyone had nothing to give to someone who had previously been an addict and a gambler. Nobody wanted to give anything to someone they had not talked to in a while and who contacted them only when he was in need.

I sat in the hallway, my head clutched in my hands, my phone was broken at the end of the hall. The only money we had left was spent on her medicines. I was in massive debt already, and there was nothing of value that I could sell in a few hours.

I had to go back to my old ways.

I knew that at 8:00 in the evening on a Saturday night, I could find many undeserving rich kids in alleys smoking, loaded with cash. The doctors told me I had only an hour, I needed only half of it.

On a quick trip from my house to the most crowded part of the town, I was armed with a gun, to scare, and a mask to cower behind.

I was right. There was a lot of young mindless sheep, validating their existence with the substance that was taking their undeserving life away. I would never let my children do this, ever. I had done gang robberies in the past, so it was easy to target, but I was alone and my partners in crime were all serving in jail.

I had to find a lone wolf. And that's when I saw her, standing at the end of the darkest and the emptiest alley, looking at me with a face that was a façade to cover her hollowness.

Going through the maze of people, I quietly took out my mask and entered the alley. No one was close by, and the silence was eerie and suffocating. Blood rushed to my face and the face of my wife came in front of me.

"We got lucky, babe, we got another chance. Don't mess this up ever," she said as we started our life with a new name, and got clean of drugs.

I am doing this for her. This is our only chance. I don't have time to waste. Love is an emotion where rationality cedes its primacy to passion.

I looked around one more time and then looked at her, whose back was facing me. Did she know I am here? Her attire screamed rich.

She turned to look at me, and I raised my gun, saying the same line to her I had to a million people over the years.

"Give me what you have, and I will not kill you. You scream, and you are dead," I said, hoping she couldn't hear the shaking of my voice.

She was not surprised. I wondered if I screwed up with an undercover cop. And then, she unlatched her watch and threw it towards me. Her wallet, necklace, and earrings followed next. Everything I could ever need was lying at my feet, but how could it be this easy?

I scrunched my eyebrows in confusion, searching her face. She had nothing in those eyes. Her face was a blank canvas, and even the layers of make-up could not cover the vacant look that resided there. It was not an act of courage, but I could feel the intimidation rising in crimson shades, hidden behind my mask.

And then she started moving towards me. Slowly, but lifelessly. Her heels touching the gravel were like knells coming nearer and nearer. Every time her heels clicked, it felt like a ticking bomb about to explode. I wanted to scream at her to stay back, but nothing came out of my mouth. The way she walked, showed that she was not going to fight me, and it made me even more anxious. Daze started to take over me, and I wanted to see what she wanted. She stood right in front of me. Taller than me. My gun touched right where her heart was, and I wondered if it was beating in this lifeless mannequin of clay.

She put her stone-cold hands over my trembling hands, and in a swift motion pulled the trigger. As she fell to the floor, her blood ran over all the stuff she had thrown. As the last ounces of life left her eyes, my world toppled. Her body went limp, and my mind stopped working.

I experienced my first panic attack. I expected to be choking on the ground, or shaking until my insides poured out. It was nothing like that. My mind was screaming, my heart was beating, my body was shivering, but none of them were connected anymore. I could breathe, but every breath that I took was a stab to my heart. Every memory that swarmed my mind started pulling my soul out of my body like removing a cloth from a bed of needles. I wondered if I had dreamt it all, and I had been shot myself. I wondered if I was lying dead on that cold street, in a miserable pool of my own blood. I wondered if this was hell, and my punishment was an imprisonment in my own clay coffin.

I could hear the sirens, I could feel someone screaming at me, someone handcuffing me, someone taking me to a dark van, but all I could think was nothing. Everything was out of my mind, but there was only one sound clouding my thoughts. A pair of heels clicking with the ground.

"She was fighting too much so I had to kill her. I did not think, and it happened impulsively," I said, unaware of anything my lawyer asked me before. I couldn't understand what he said after either.

Everything aside, how could I tell anyone that she had killed herself? I might as well go to jail with a badge on my shoulder, instead of a crazy story starting a gossip in every room.

"My wife?" I asked him, a confirmation for something I already knew. I could feel it in my gut. I knew she had left. There was a chill in my bones, an absence of the warmth that was invoked by her presence.

He sighed and shook his head in dismay. I lost my three reasons to live. I knew it well before this confirmation that I had.

A part of me was happy to be convicted, for I had a place to eat, sleep and an ease to remember my wife. As that girl snatched her freedom from me, she extricated me from the loneliness of my life that was to come.

It wouldn't be until thirty years that I would have a visitor, and realize that my son did survive that miserable night.

Bloom with Grace
Maania Farhan

They looked at the ancient building from roof to its entrance, and contemplated whether it was the building or the surroundings that sent a shiver up their spines. It could be both, blending in with each other and creating a scary scene out of a movie. It was a three-story building made with red bricks. Most of it was covered with dead vines and creepers, some were hanging from the balconies and some had grown upwards from the ground. It wasn't dark yet, but the gate lights were on. The gate was slightly open and just when Romana grabbed her suitcase to head inside, a fat cat walked out of the house. A shriek escaped her mouth and she stepped backwards.

"Are you mad? The whole neighborhood will wake up, and it's *just* a *cat*," Narmeen glared at her friend and whispered.

"The sun hasn't even set, why would people sleep at this hour? Unless they are all dead, which seems like a possibility." Romana eyed the silent street in fear. "And do you think *this* creature coming out of *this* house could be *just* a cat?"

"Exactly my point genius." Narmeen gritted her teeth. "Do you want to wake up the dead to welcome you?" She looked at the cat who was sitting at the entrance and was leisurely licking her paws. She reminded Narmeen of a killer sharpening his knife and daring them to come inside. Narmeen didn't want to confirm Romana's fears, because at this hour they couldn't go anywhere else either.

"If you guys plan to sleep here tonight, just let me know, I'll leave your luggage here and head home."

Both girls jumped in fright. During their house inspection, they had completely forgotten about Raffey's presence. But it also reminded them that he was the one who had brought them here, and their guns turned towards him.

"This was your choice, right?" Romana poked her brother with every word. "You chose this hostel for us so that we would give up on our dreams and run away. I knew I shouldn't have trusted you!"

"Excuse me, drama queen." Raffey slapped her hand away. "I would have gladly taken credit of this noble deed upon my head if I hadn't been shocked by this place myself." He then raised his arm to her eye level, "look at my hair standing like a battalion of army officers."

"Was it your brother, Narmeen?"

"Of course, my sixteen years old brother is quite capable of traveling all the way to Lahore and book us a hostel."

"Oh, right," Romana pretended not to be affected by her sarcasm.

"*Abba Jee* chose this place for you," Raffey told them.

"But we told him to book a hostel not a haunted house in an ancient side of Lahore," Romana whined.

"One of his friends' relative owns this hostel." He grabbed a suitcase and walked towards the house. "She is a widow and..."

"I know, I know," Narmeen, who inhaled novels all day, interrupted him. "Her husband passed away and she has no children. She loved her husband so much, and as this house is his only memory, she decided not to move out. But she had to earn as well so she opened a hostel for girls. I swear it's the same story everywhere, where is the plot twist?"

"I was going to say this is a safe neighborhood," He gave her a look as he tried to cross the cat who was now laying on the ground and staring in the unknown. Raffey wondered if she was looking at a ghost, but decided not to voice his thoughts. They had already wasted a lot of time just standing there, and it was getting dark.

Narmeen and Romana followed Raffey, muttering all the prayers they had ever been taught. The house was bigger than it seemed from the outside. A lush green lawn welcomed them and gently lifted their fears like a butler would take their luggage. They didn't expect a beauty protected beneath such a haunting appearance. A guard escorted them to a small office. A tall old lady sat in the chair behind the desk. She looked like someone in her late sixties, but that could only be guessed due to the silver hair peeking from her *dupatta*. Her face was glowing with all the shades of calmness. She welcomed them and called a maid who escorted them to their room on the second floor. Raffey was sent back home and the guard carried their luggage all the way to the top floor.

The girls were too enchanted by the beauty of the place to speak. Both of them preferred observing the *haveli* over talking. The high ceilings made them feel small, and the antique furniture too young. The lush abandoned army area at the back of the *haveli* dared them to leave the window and go to their beds. They gladly accepted the challenge and collapsed. They had four years to explore this *haveli,* and embrace its warmth. It reminded them of their own *haveli* back in their village. Their feelings had turned into a sweet smoothie upon which they had gleefully gotten drunk on and fallen into a deep slumber.

The next few days went by adjusting to the place. In their free time they explored the *haveli* as if it called out to them, or simply drooled over its interior. Romana had come to Lahore to study interior designing, while Narmeen had gotten admission in architectural engineering. Both best friends had found it in their best interest to explore the not so huge *haveli*, and memorise its each and every dimension. The front lawn was their favorite part of the house but for different reasons. For Romana, it was the rope swing tied to the widespread banyan tree in the middle of the lawn. Narmeen found sitting in the lawn and reading quite relaxing. The feeling that they were on vacation had clung to them, and both feared they might find it too hard to set a routine when their classes would start.

"I see you like reading,"

Narmeen, who was deeply invested in a novel, looked up, startled. Safia aunty, their hostel owner and warden, stood across from her. Her face was glowing and her smile was radiating a warmth that always made their hearts melt like Dairy Milk in summers. Romana, who had already seen Safia aunty approaching them, left the swing and greeted her. They took their seats and Safia aunty repeated her statement.

"Yes," Narmeen smiled sheepishly, "but only novels."

"It is a good hobby," Safia aunty nodded, "but why only novels? Why not history or something more realistic?"

Narmeen hesitated. She loved talking about novels but her mouth turned bitter every time someone, specifically an elder, expressed that novels spoiled girls. She tried to reply as respectfully as she could.

"Stories make me feel productive, I learn from them."

"Stories, are lies." Safia aunty's voice was soft and encouraging.

"Stories teach you about reality."

"So does history, and non-fictional books."

"Not every person learns the same way. Some digest harsh realities quicker, while others learn from realities disguised in sweet stories."

"I like how confident you are about your choice of reading," Safia aunty's smile broadened, she looked impressed and proud. "It speaks how there are more than just stories for you in these books. An endless ocean of words and lessons. Reminds me of my youth."

"Did you read novels too?" Romana leaned forward, surprised.

"Not novels," Safia aunty shook her head, "history. I was born in the year our country was freed. I grew curious what had happened that year which made my parents wonder if they should throw me in a well during migration."

"Do you remember about migration?" Romana was on the edge of her chair with excitement and curiosity.

"Seriously, Romana?" Narmeen looked at her like someone would look at a child when they asked an idiotic question.

"No," Safia aunty chuckled, "I was only three months old."

"Oh," Romana said, now understanding the look in her friend's eyes.

"Did you ever feel that maybe you don't belong here, maybe you should have been there, across the border, where you and your parents were born?" Narmeen asked.

Ever since she had moved into the hostel, she had asked herself this question many times. Living away from her family had seemed exciting only for a few days. Later on, she felt like she was divided into two, her roots were somewhere else, longing to be united with its tree which was thrown somewhere far.

"What is the feeling of belongingness?" Safia aunty answered her question with a question.

"It's the feeling that you are at the right place, your feet are rooted deep inside the ground there. They are not bare, making you weak and vulnerable."

"You are not wrong," Safia aunty agreed, "but to me, it's spreading my roots in whichever soil God plants me in. I have to water myself and nourish myself. Not with tears but with sweat of hard work. Belongingness is making your place rather than looking for it. I grew in the soil of Amritsar, god gently pulled me out of there and planted me in Barisal. From there I was sent to Lahore. There is a French proverb which might explain it better for you,"

"Wherever life plants you, bloom with grace."

"Life taught me that wherever I am I have to bloom with grace. Its soil won't accept me till I won't embrace it."

Safia aunty paused, and as if on cue, the prayer-call for *Maghreb* raised from the nearby mosque. They had been too invested in the conversation to notice the sky changing its shades to a deep purple.

"Allah u Akbar," Safia aunty got up slowly in surprise, "we should prepare for *Salah*. See you at dinner."

Both girls nodded, still deep in thought, and watched aunty leave.

"Narmeen?" Romana called her friend, who was still deep in thought from the conversation, as they headed inside.

"Hmm?"

"Remember the plot twist you asked about when we came here?"

"Yeah,"

"I think this was it." Romana shrugged and left her friend to be thrilled by the sudden plot twists in the story.

Cracks of Time
Zobia Arif

Escorted by the railway police on the train station, a woman in her mid-thirties became the subject of the gaze of a dozen men and women. Her eyes caught hold of "Passport Verification office Delhi" written on the plate outside a small dingy room. Following the police officer, she entered it. Behind the table with dusty pile of files on one side and an empty cup of tea on the other, was sitting a middle aged man. His bulky body covered with crisp ironed shirt made the chair he was sitting on lean backwards. "She's from Pakistan... wants to go to Dhaka," said the man who brought her in. The words brought a murkiness on the face of the man sitting behind the table. "Pakistan..." he leaned forward with a creek in his chair. "Adab! What's your good name, Mohtarma?" The woman, clenching her beige cotton saree, replied in a quirky voice, "Sakeena... Sakeena Alam."

"So, Sakeena bibi what is making you travel to Bangladesh from Pakistan, all alone?" the officer asked with a hint of mistrust in his tone. "I'm going back home, my roots are from Dhaka, the boundaries fortified me in a land unknown," her voice almost cracked up while speaking those words. Your passport is new, why didn't you go back earlier?" The question ignited turmoil of emotions bringing back the memories of countless trips she made to the Indian and Bengal Embassy. A lone woman in a foreign land, trying to get through the never ending visa process, in such uncertain times. With her mind racing, she explained yet another time when her husband, a military officer, passed away in a crossfire between Pakistan and India on the line of control.

Lacking the resources and due to ongoing tensions between the countries, she was only able to get her passport nineteen years after the independence of Bangladesh.

The nearby loudspeakers announced that Maitree Express was ready for departure from platform number nine. It was her train. Her years long struggle to reach back home. She asked the guard the quickest way to the platform and was on her way. She heard the final horn of the train indicating the last call for passengers, when she stepped onto the train. She walked through the dim lit corridor, looking for the compartment number mentioned on her ticket. The passage leading to her compartment was filled with a mixed smell of travelers from far off places, sweating in mid-June heat and air filled with a sensation of longing. The passengers had the common look of waiting for what was there to come when they reach their destinations. She settled down in an all women compartment at the end of the train.

The moving scenery outside the window played with her memories like an old VCR cassette being rewinded into time. Sitting in the backyard of her childhood home, situated somewhere on one of the unpaved streets of Dhaka, she braided the hair of her twin sister, Haseena. Above them, an Almond tree was blooming with flowers. The slight breeze made a flower fall into Haseena's lap. "Oh I want this," Sakeena exclaimed. Haseena turned around and her eyes were sparkling with desire. "I'll give you this flower if you get me a bowl of kheer," she said. Sakeena ran into the kitchen and spent next few hours making the desired dish. She came back with the bowl having sweet aroma of love, "Now the flower?" she demanded. This tiny action became a beloved ritual; whenever Haseena wanted something from her sister, she'd bring her a flower from that very almond tree. For the love of both the flower and her sister she couldn't refuse.

Her trail of thoughts was disrupted by the beat of dholak and women singing wedding songs, she realised that a groom's family was travelling with her. The happy songs made her sing along those women until there was silence in the compartment and she was the only one singing. "Oh... your voice is so melodious," a woman, sitting across from her exclaimed. This made her conscious of her surroundings and she stopped. The women asked from where did she learn to sing so good. She looked out of the window as if she was finding the answer in those passing fields, her mind raced back to the time spent in her childhood home again. She could see herself skipping in her house, singing songs she learnt from the old women of the neighbourhood, songs she picked up at weddings, songs she heard on radio, songs she used to sing with her sister. "Ah! My mother had a beautiful voice, maybe I got it from her," she almost whispered, "one of those things my father couldn't allow me," her eyes watered. "What?" asked the woman beside her and Sakeena went quite. Her eyes caught the sight of those always moving clock hands, it was half past three. She never understood the idea of clocks because she thought that time never really changes.

"Where is Haseena?" their father yelled. The sisters thought it was one of the many outbursts of their father, little did they know it was the night when their lives were going to change forever. "Tell her to come out of the room," he shouted again. They walked nearer so the shadows of their feet were visible from under the door. "Just listen to me Haseena. You have an hour to pack your things. I've arranged your wedding with Ijaaz, the carpenter's son. He is an army officer. You don't have to ask the reason why. You'll do it because I, your father told you so." The girls trembled with fear. His habit of gambling had caused the loss of all their household items and now this. His command made the ground under Haseena's feet shake. A sixteen-year-old, seeing all her dreams of going for higher studies shatter.

Sakeena loved her sister a little too much to let that happen. "She'll not go anywhere," she yelled back from behind the door. The father insisted, "The people will be here in an hour." Sakeena busted out of the room defending her sister. "You marry him then," the words came out as a spear in her heart. The silence echoed for some moments till she uttered, "I will." Haseena protested but the father was already gone to get those men. Meanwhile the sisters held onto each other and cried. Sakeena walked to the Almond tree and picked a flower. Bringing it to her sister, she said, "All my life I've fulfilled all your wishes for this flower, this time I'm asking you to fulfil one for me." The sobs muffled the broken words, "I want you to study, don't let him tear you, I just want one wish... Years from now, I want to see you prospering." The next thing they knew was that there were men in their house, a small wedding ritual and Sakeena was being taken away. The air was filled with Haseena's cries, calling out her sister's name.

Sakeena jolted up from her memory due to the calling of an old Bengali woman from the adjacent berth. The realisation that she was dreaming about that night again struck her. "We'll reach Dhaka in 20 minutes," the woman told her.

Upon reaching Dhaka, she took a taxi ride to her childhood home, the sun was going down and even the magnificently painted sky couldn't calm her heart. After nineteen long years, she was back on her own soil, she didn't know what to expect but her heart had a frail hope. The taxi stopped outside the gate of the old house, it looked more bleak and rusty than how she last remembered it to be. The moment she touched it, she felt the years escaping. The last time she saw that door was when she was leaving with that man. She felt something inside her coming to life, something she thought was long dead, her heart swelled up with both, relief and angst at the same time.

The door was open, she walked inside and it appeared as if it was abandoned, the blooming almond tree of her childhood was now just a dried up trunk and branches. Dead leaves accumulated in the corners. Throughout her journey she had thought of all possible scenarios and an abandoned house felt one of them. Then she heard some coughing, that's when she realized that the light of the back room was switched on. She walked into the room and saw just a broken charpai and a feeble looking man on it. It was her father. He looked at the door in silence and then broke into tears. "Is it you Sakeena? Is it really you," he said. She knew that time had taken things from her that couldn't be replaced. "I am here for Haseena. Where is she?" she replied.

The next morning the sun was blindingly sharp. Sakeena sat beside the gravestone in a desolate state. She held the mud in her fists and cried. "Hey, how have you been... Look I've come back for you." The tiredness and grief pierced her heart so she lied beside Haseena's grave. She hummed the song they used to sing together but this loss felt too much. "I don't want to sing alone, not ever," she spoke while closing her eyes. Rahat Ara Jahan School for Music Learning was engraved onto a wooden plate hung outside the red brick building. Melodies of love and loss could be heard while standing outside the windows of the school. "I'll go there someday," Sakeena exclaimed.

The scorching heat woke her up. She said her goodbye to her sister who died of consumption a year before. Walking out of the graveyard, preoccupied with the thought of the music school she saw in her dream, a flower fell on the ground. A flower from an Almond tree, she picked it up and tears rolled down her eyes. Time took her on unimaginably hostile paths, all of them unknown but this time she knew where she was going.

SHORT STORIES FROM
THE UNITED STATES

The Origin Tree
Lloyd David Aquino

I. The Origin Tree

Where is the once blushing-bride-to-be?
She's gone below, swallowed by the sea.
And her quiet husband; where is he?
High above, in the Origin Tree,
He's waiting for his love in the Origin Tree.

The children's song was interrupted only by fits of giggles. Bits of treeskin, yellowed and paper-thin, danced to the ground, only to be crushed by the children's feet. Though all the children of the village were there, they could not hold hands and form a complete circle around the Origin Tree, so thick was its trunk.

Benjie could hear neither the roar of the sea nor the children's song. From where he sat, there was only one sound, so familiar in its repetition.

Scrape. Scrape. Scrape. Scrape.

Sitting atop the thickest branch of the Origin Tree, the oldest and tallest narra tree in the village, Benjie glanced down. It was now dusk and the children had finally been called home. Benjie wiped the sweat from his face, felt more sweat trickle down the back of his neck as wind brushed past him. The sea murmured, and Benjie returned to his work.

Scrape. Scrape. Scrape. Scrape.

When Benjie had first climbed the Origin Tree (and a long and difficult task it had been), it had not been long before the village children, who had been playing one of their many games nearby, had run back to tell the elders. In fact, he was still struggling to reach the topmost canopy when he heard the first strains of outrage as the elders approached, followed by the children and anyone else who had no responsibilities to keep them busy (and even some who did).

Come down from there, foolish boy!

Benjie had kept climbing, losing his footing for a brief, terrible moment when the treebark cracked beneath his foot. Fortunately, a thin branch somehow bore his weight. Breathing a sigh of relief, he ignored the commands shouted up at him, and the sudden scrapes and cuts that appeared on his arms and legs, and the splinters digging into his fingers. It went on like this for some time, the sunlight around him disappearing in the growing thickness of the Origin Tree.

Disrespectful boy! Listen to your elders!

No one had ever dared to climb the Origin Tree. According to legend, which adults had told children for many generations, the Origin Tree had birthed all other narra, so treasured by the people of the village, who even kept miniature ones inside their homes. And so the Origin Tree was treated with great reverence; indeed, from every generation a select few were chosen and trained to tend to its every need, a station held in the highest regard, for many in the village (though few would ever voice it) believed that their happiness and well-being would turn rotten like unharvested bananas if the Origin Tree were ever to perish.

Come down so we can punish you!

Benjie cared little about punishments. He simply bit down harder on the wooden handle of his knife, given to him by his father some years ago to gut the fresh catch carried home every day, and continued climbing. He supposed he could have said something to calm the elders, but he did not feel like lying, and he suspected that the true reason for his climbing the Origin Tree would not satisfy them. So he said nothing, but bit down harder on the handle of his knife. He spotted the thickest branch, and so breathed another sigh of relief now that the end of his ascent was within sight. The muscles and bones beneath his skin would only need to burn a little while longer.

Down below, the elders had begun to realize the futility of their threats. They ordered the children to wait at the foot of the tree, then returned to the village, grumbling and muttering their anger at one another and to anyone who would listen. *Just wait*, they swore, *until that disrespectful boy comes back down.* And though they had no idea what punishment they would inflict upon Benjie, each of them looked forward to that moment.

Since that day, no one in the village had seen hide nor hair of Benjie, not since he had disappeared into the darkness of the Origin Tree's canopy, for Benjie never came down. The children returned to the foot of the tree every morning to play their games and sing their songs, and as each night approached, the fishermen and their wives shuffled past, heading towards or returning from the shore. After dinner, there were always a few adults milling about for reasons they did not care to share with anyone else. And still no one had seen Benjie.

How does he eat? What does he drink? Everyone had adopted their own story. The most popular was that he ate bark and leaves and drank the sap from the Origin Tree. *And what does he do up there all day?* The only clues they were given were the bits of treeskin that now surrounded the foot of the tree, which had been falling since Benjie's ascent. Some bits had begun to drift into the village, perhaps carried by the wind, perhaps not. But no one could decipher these paper-thin pieces of wood, and no one considered climbing up after Benjie. It was forbidden, after all, and besides, it was such a long and difficult task for even the strongest villager. *Not worth the effort*, the villagers grumbled. *Just wait until he comes down,* the elders assured one another.

And so in time the villagers came to accept Benjie's antics as a normal part of their lives and stopped asking questions, just as they had always done whenever some disaster struck, like the Fire, or the Flood, or the Drought.

II. The Night Before

Wait for me.

Benjie could feel the smile on Tala's lips as she whispered into his ear. The other villagers had begun to disperse, moving as one towards the home of Tala's parents, where abundant bowls of fish, rice and giant, overflowing jugs of pineapple and coconut juice awaited them. For the moment, they were alone and forgotten. She let out a little breath as she moved away, and he felt it brush past him. His hand found hers as she turned to go. *Don't be long,* the gesture said.

My love. She stared at him for a moment, her fig leaf eyes shining. *My husband. Wait for me.*

Standing beneath the Origin Tree, where every marriage ceremony in the village took place, he watched her go, never losing sight even in the growing darkness, as she moved closer and closer to the shore and the small boat waiting for her. And he knew the exact moment when she turned to look back at him before entering the boat, followed in a second, larger boat by her mother, her sister, aunts and female cousins.

He knew they were heading out to make offerings to Limat, god of the sea, but Benjie had only a faint idea of the rituals Tala would perform by herself, such were the secrets that women kept. They would be back soon, and the sooner he joined the wedding banquet, the sooner their return would be. He would endure the half-hearted congratulations from each of Tala's would-be suitors, the blessings heaped upon him by the elders of the village, and the drunken singing of his relatives, and they would return before he grew tired of all the unwanted attention, and Tala would be at his side.

Still, at the home of Tala's parents, Benjie quickly grew disinterested in the musicians strumming their guitars and banging their agongs, or in the children singing songs he had forgotten he once knew. The elders' stories bored him, and the idle gossip of the other village women only made him feel more and more restless. He had not touched the fish and rice heaped in front of him, nor the drinks offered in congratulations by his father and uncles. In his mind, he was sitting in the boat, holding Tala, letting his fingers slip through her long black hair, then fall to her bare arms, which he tickled gently by tracing his fingertips up and down in perfect unison with the half-slumbering waves rocking them back and forth.

Then gradually his waking dream changed shape, and he saw himself sitting with his back against the Origin Tree, Tala leaning back against him as she hummed, her eyes half-closed as the skin of her bare arms tingled at the touch of Benjie's fingertips. Lowering his chin to rest atop the hollow of her shoulder, Benjie breathed a sigh into her neck, causing her to shiver just a little bit.

Tell me a story, she said.

Above, the thick canopy of the Origin Tree rustled and shook like rainfall.

Please, Benjie. A story.

But Benjie did not know any stories and told her so. She laughed at that, sending a pleasant sensation through Benjie's chest.

Tell me a story anyway.

And so Benjie told her of the only time his father had taken him out on his fishing boat. He was eleven. The ocean was silent and still. Motionless. For a long while, the only sound was his father's humming as he minded the nets. And Benjie leaned over the side and stared at his reflection in the clear blue water.

Impossible.

No. The ocean was silent and still.

Motionless.

Yes. And Benjie could see his reflection so clearly.

What did you see?

Benjie could feel himself fumbling for good words. Tala giggled again. *And so serious. You're always so serious.*

She took his face. She took it in her hands. The warmth of her palms made him smile. *What happened next?*

Nothing. Benjie's father dragged the net up to the surface, and his reflection shattered. Like glass. The fish flapped, gasping for the sea. The net was heavy. Benjie could not even lift his end. And his father stopped humming.

There was a long silence. The sound of rainfall was gone. Benjie breathed, careful not to disturb a hair on Tala's head. Her charcoal colored head, and her skin, soft like paper.

You are a bad storyteller. She took his face. And kissed him.

That was the day he had asked Tala to marry him, and now he opened his eyes, or so it seemed, for in fact they had remained open the whole time, the mere handful of seconds that had passed.

Instantly came the wailing that shattered his happiness like glass, a terrible sound that silenced everyone. The revelers watched as the women came inside. Tala's mother, barely held up by all of Tala's aunts. It was her wailing that they had heard. And Tala's sister and cousins, each of them sobbing in silence. For a long while, Benjie and the other men could only wait, though Benjie knew long before anyone said a word.

Finally, one of Tala's aunts spoke. How Tala's boat and their own could not push past the crushing waves, how their boat had been overturned, how it had taken them longer than they could say to gather everyone up and into the boat again. How, breathless and shivering, they had accounted for everyone.

Except Tala. (And now all eyes turned to Benjie.) Her boat was nowhere to be seen, no matter how they strained their eyes and their throats in hopes of some sign.

Benjie could not remember what happened after, or perhaps he did not care to. For days, Tala's face was all he saw, and Tala's last words to him were all he heard. *Wait for me. Wait for me. Wait for me...*

He did not leave his parents' home for many days. No food or drink passed his lips. He did not speak. He sat alone day and night, looking in the direction of the great, terrible ocean. But always the Origin Tree stood in his way.

III. Work to Be Done

It was not long before the rumors began to spread through the village like some infection of the mouth. The disease seemed to strike each person differently, for there were nearly as many stories as there were villagers. Then the stories began to harden like drying tree sap, and the village could be split into groups according to the rumor being advocated. Many of the elders, for example, believed Tala had been dragged into the depths by the Bakunawa as payment for his generosity in allowing the fishermen to sail safely and prosper in his waters. The young women, many of whom had once claimed to be Tala's friend, whispered to one another that she had run away to the arms of an unknown lover (*A nobleman from another island,* they decided, *someone of great wealth*), and that she had never wished to marry Benjie, who they thought was strange and unattractive, and that her parents had arranged the marriage without her consent. The fishermen scoffed at such stories and assured one another that the young girl had simply drowned, the waves' tight grip too strong to struggle against and survive.

Others thought to themselves, but never said aloud, that she was still sailing the seas, trying to find her way home.

Then, of course, there was the children's song.

> *Where is the blushing-bride-to-be?*
> *Some would say she's lost at sea.*
> *And her would-be husband; where is he?*
> *Waiting at his doorstep quietly,*
> *Waiting for his lost bird to return to her tree.*

Benjie heard them all when finally he emerged from his parents' home, ignoring the surprise spilling from his mother's lips. It was scarcely dawn, the sky the color of ube, the sun a mere shadow of itself. But Benjie shuffled past her, stopping for only a half-breath to pick up his knife.

He did not stop to drink in the delicious breeze splashing against his face, rustling the unruly hair he had allowed to grow far longer than usual. Instead, he began walking purposefully towards the Origin Tree. He knew that he was expected to go out fishing with his father and the other men of the village, that he was no longer a child and therefore needed to learn the family trade. He half-remembered his father's chiding in those days after Tala's disappearance.

Now is the time to stop lying about and do your part, his father would say. *There is work to be done.*

And there was. But not on any boat, not hauling in nets and rowing against tide. He knew with every fiber of his being that he would never take on his father's trade, that indeed he was never meant to do such work. As Benjie crossed the heart of the village, he ignored the surprised stares of the villagers and only half-heard the murmured rumors. He paid them no mind. There was work to be done.

And so he climbed.

IV. The Guardians

Several weeks after Benjie's ascent, the whispers of quiet complaint steadily grew to the size of muttered outrage, then to louder and louder cries for punishment.

The Origin Tree has been desecrated, more and more voices began to shout during the village meetings, *and still we do nothing!* Even those once sympathetic towards Benjie, those who had themselves lost a loved one sometime ago, began to feel a kind of bitterness rising in their throats, like calamansi left half-swallowed.

The elders soon selected four of the most obedient and vigilant young men of the village, and ordered them to stand watch over the Origin Tree each and every night and apprehend Benjie at first sight. Meanwhile, the four young men would train during the day by climbing every banyan and narra and every coconut and banana tree surrounding the village. Once they had climbed to the very top of one, they would start the task of climbing the next tallest. Though each of these young men possessed some physical strength and no small amount of courage, soon enough they were complaining to one another about the difficulty of this task, and wondering how in the world Benjie had accomplished it, and why in the world they were expected to learn to do the same. The trunk of the Origin Tree was too thick, its treebark too brittle. However, they did not dare to say such things whenever an elder was present.

If that foolish boy won't come down, the elders said to one another, *then we will send them up there to get him.*

Upon hearing of the elders' proclamation, the people of the village were confident that it would not be long before this whole strange ordeal came to an end and things returned to a state of normalcy. One way or another, Benjie would be caught and punished, and that would be the end of that. Some even kept the four young guardians company during those first few nights, or else shouted out words of encouragement as they trained during the day. But as more time passed with no announcement of success, their confidence began to falter, and soon enough, the people of the village seemed to forget all about the elders' proclamation and even, sadly, the young guardians. Even the question of how Benjie survived up in that treetop day after day faded from their minds.

Of course, the answer to that question was simple, perhaps so much so that even the thought of it had never occurred to anyone.

Each night, the four young guardians would gather around the Origin Tree and begin their watch. And at midnight, Benjie's mother would arrive, for she had been chosen as a child to tend to its every need. And each time, she would bring with her a pot of broth to be shared by the four guardians, who would always eat obediently and heartily, then drift to sleep as the herbs Benjie's mother always mixed in eventually, inevitably took their effect. Then with the empty pot she would tap against the trunk of the tree three times to signal her son, who would climb down (Benjie's mother never failed to notice the growing strength in her son's arms and legs, shaped by his many journeys up and down the Origin Tree) and walk with her back to their home, where he would eat as much fish and rice as he could stomach, mother and son talking quietly so that his father would not awaken from his slumber.

Sometimes, as she warmed that night's meal, waiting until after her husband had drifted off to sleep, Benjie's mother contemplated a disturbing thought. What Benjie had done should have angered her more than anyone. She, more than anyone, had just cause to harbor such a fire in her belly. After all, it was her responsibility to watch over the Origin Tree, and it was her son who challenged the beliefs she coveted so dearly. The sting should have run deeper in her veins.

And yet, strangely, Benjie's mother felt nothing of the sort. Neither did she feel even a pinch of remorse for the deception she and Benjie had devised before he had climbed the Origin Tree. Quite the opposite, actually, for what rumbled in her chest was the same feeling of pride she had felt so many years ago, when she had been Benjie's age and the elders had appointed her to her station. And, though she could never voice it to anyone – not even her own husband – she realized that her pride grew each night when she saw her son's feet touch the ground and they walked home in the twilight together.

This did not mean she had no questions, however. In fact, every night, as she stirred the sleeping herbs into the broth, she determined to ask her son a simple, yet important question: *Why?* It seemed such a strange way to spend one's days, up there in the upper reaches of the Origin Tree while everyone else went about the work of the village. He could be chopping wood, or minding a garden, or tending livestock, or hunting, or gathering. Or, according to tradition, he could be fishing with his father. (But, no, she could understand why Benjie had no interest in going out to sea.) And yet he chose...

The question would bother her each night as she carried the broth to the guardians, but then she would see her son's face. Often he wore the same look of exhaustion that his father, her husband, wore after a hard day at sea. Sometimes he would be so full of energy, his eyes would be so wide they seemed likely to jump out of his head, spurred by some unknown and unseen force. And rarely, very rarely, he would be smiling. No matter the expression, the sight of her son would cause the question to disappear from her mind, like the steam from her sleep potion curling into nothingness in the evening air. After all, he was her son, and he was coming home, at least for a little while.

Your father, she quietly announced one night, *has been taking your cousin Jejomar out fishing.*

Benjie nodded, his eyes watching the steam curling up from his bowl of rice. He blew out a bit of air, and the steam rushed away like a wave toppling and collapsing upon itself. He chewed the fish, silently wishing his mother had remembered to add some spices when she had cooked. But he said nothing.

As much as they both complain when they return home, I can tell they get along well enough.

Benjie dunked his bowl into the bucket of water, swirling it back and forth to shake loose the stray bits of rice. The water cascaded against the wood, some of it spilling over onto the floor. His father's heavy breathing emerged from out of the darkness, and Benjie froze, letting the bowl sink to the bottom of the bucket. It did not make a sound.

How many times have I told you? his mother chided him. *Your father would not wake if the heavens came tumbling down on his head. Now tell me. How many more nights must this continue?*

Benjie retrieved the bowl, carefully pouring out the water that it had collected back into the bucket, then shook the bowl dry and handed it to her. She placed it with the others. *No more,* he told her. He only needed one more day to finish his work.

Benjie's mother picked up the bucket, which was ready to be dumped into the grass outside. *Your work. I suppose this means you'll finally tell me what this work of yours is. Because you should hear what people are saying—*

But when she turned around again, Benjie was gone.

IV. The End

Benjie stopped his work, taking a moment to study his ragged, calloused hands in the half-light of the waking sun.

Below, he could hear the guardians just awakening. He took out the piece of sandstone he kept in his pocket and moved it about the giant trunk of the Origin Tree, smoothing the surface. Its old bark had long been stripped away, leaving pale skin where once there was dark like charcoal. As he continued his work, he began to hum the melody of the children's song. Moving the sandstone in the patterns he had fashioned and memorized over time, Benjie's humming turned into a chant, mouthed and no louder than a sigh.

Where is my Tala who married me?
She's lost at sea and waiting for me,
Her would-be husband, and where is he?
Waiting for her in the Origin Tree,
Waiting for her to call out to me.

By dusk, the sun was about to disappear into the thickness of the canopy, and Benjie laid down his knife and sandstone. Leaning his back against the trunk of the ancient, ageless tree, Benjie gazed at the work that had taken him... days, he knew, but beyond that, time had collapsed on itself and become immeasurable. Nevertheless, it was finally done.

As nightfall swept across the sky, blanketing it with stars, Benjie sidled across the thick branch that had held his weight all this time, moving slowly and carefully to its edge. As he did, his body began to emerge from the topmost canopy and almost glow in the first vestiges of moonlight. Nearing the edge of the branch, he watched as the ocean, looking so calm from this distance, repeated its endless rhythm, scarcely aware of his watchful eye.

Every morning...

Benjie's thoughts began to drift, and once again he was leaning against the Origin Tree, Tala again resting in his arms and humming.

Every morning, he suddenly said to her, causing her to stop, *we sit beneath this same tree, and I listen to you hum the same songs.*

Tala turned her head a bit, her fig leaf eyes peering into his own.

The same every morning. And it was only today that I realized I could live a lifetime of these mornings, so long as you are here with me.

Tala giggled softly. *You're being silly.*

Benjie sighed through his own smile. *Every morning, for as long as I live.*

His skin tingled as she nestled her head into his chest. *Every morning,* she repeated, her voice scarcely more than a whisper. *Silly boy.*

A strong gale woke Benjie from his half-slumber, and he clutched at the branch anew. When had that happened? Benjie realized he could not recall. It did not matter. His work was done.

Then something strange happened. Everything fell silent. No longer could he hear the sea's murmurings, or the children's song, or the guardians' footsteps below. Benjie dared to move just a bit further down the edge of the branch, straining his ears to catch some sound. But not even the branch creaked in protest, and he could not even hear himself breathe or his heart beat. All was still.

V. Honesto and the Woman in the Wood

It was Benjie's mother who sounded the alarm, for she had gone to the Origin Tree at midnight, and fed the guardians their broth, and tapped the tree trunk three times. But Benjie had not come down. She tapped again and waited, then did so again, each time a bit more insistent than before. When finally she had rushed back and awoken the village elders, now accompanied by her bleary-eyed husband, and told them everything, everyone hurried at once to the Origin Tree.

They shook awake the four guardians, then Benjie's mother and father called his name over and over again. Still Benjie did not appear, and his voice could not be heard. Soon enough, it was decided that the oldest and strongest of the four guardians would climb the Origin Tree. (This was followed by some time spent encouraging the reluctant young man that he could indeed accomplish this feat, and then convincing him that he would not be punished for it.) It was a long, arduous climb that took nearly half the day. The sun disappeared into the thick canopy as the elders and Benjie's parents arched their heads upwards, ignoring the protestations of their muscles and joints. They could no longer see Honesto, the young guardian who had been chosen, though they could hear the scraping of skin against bark and the ever fainter grunts.

Tell us what you see!

Honesto was too focused on his task to reply. The sun continued its downward spiral, seeking again its ocean sanctuary. Honesto made it to the thickest, strongest branch of the Origin Tree. Weakly, awkwardly, he heaved his body onto it. He breathed in and thought he smelled burnt wood. At that moment, no other thought entered his mind except that simple command: breathe. He did not think of the growing ache in his wrists and under his fingernails, nor of the sweat stinging his eyes shut.

And so he did not think about Benjie at first. And neither did he notice the knife.

There it was, inches from where he had laid his head, embedded in the thickest, strongest branch. It was Benjie's knife, and it glistened in the half-light. Honesto did not squint. Something about the sight filled him with an unease that he would never be able to describe, even years later. Half of him wanted to reach out and remove the knife, convinced that this action would correct that wrong he sensed but could not name. But the other half gave him pause. And so he stared for a long time, even as the voices of the elders reached him, demanding to know what he saw.

As if prompted by some trick of the light, Honesto's silent stare shifted from Benjie's knife to the view beyond, and he saw what Benjie had seen for longer than anyone could bother to remember – what only Benjie had seen until now.

It was the ocean. And yet it was not the ocean Honesto had known, not the ocean he had bathed and played in as a child, and not the ocean he would one day travel in his father's fishing boat, years from now when he had children and grandchildren of his own. Honesto found that he could neither breathe nor move, so beautiful was the sight before him, so vast and infinite and unknowable. Finally, he pried his eyes away by turning his head just slightly.

And there she was.

She sat leaning against the great trunk of the Origin Tree, nothing more than a shadow in the deepening dusk gloom. Honesto leaned in, clutching the branch tightly.

She sat with her legs crossed and her arms meeting at the palms, her fingers tangled together in her lap. She was smiling at him, the curves of her cheeks dimpled, her nose crinkled. Her skin was the color of paper left to yellow for a moment too long in the sun. And, impossibly, her hair was a deep shade of black covering her shoulders; a stray strand had even settled against her left cheek.

The white dress she wore draped across her perfectly.

Honesto resisted the urge to cry out her name, to rush to her side, to let loose the thousands of questions he had heard everyone in the village utter since that night. But he knew she would not respond. Slowly, he began crawling toward her, ignoring the jagged bark scraping his knees.

Every curve of her matched perfectly his memory of her, but she did not move as he approached. Instead, her eyes stared straight ahead, past Honesto, through him, at the sea beyond. As he came closer, he could now see the individual strands of hair that had been carved so carefully. He could now see that her hair and eyes had been colored using pieces of charcoal. Making sure not to graze her yellow paper skin, he examined her more closely, noting the veins so scarcely visible, yet there they were, carved so expertly by some gentle, careful hand.

And though he knew she would never protest, he understood that he was not meant to see her. He was nothing more than an intruder. The skin at the back of his neck shivered as he moved back to take in the sight one last time.

It was night when he finally appeared to the villagers again, his legs emerging first from the darkness of the canopy. The elders, many of whom had long grown hoarse shouting, grumbled now about how an entire day had been wasted. Before Honesto's feet had touched the ground, they were upon him, a cacophony of old crows cawing their incessant song – or so it seemed now to him. He said nothing as he walked home, no longer hearing their orders, which receded into rebukes, then finally curses. The message was clear to those few, such as Benjie's parents, who were willing to listen.

The elders were furious at Honesto's disobedience and cursed the younger generation and its growing disrespect. Silently, as if resigned to their darkest thoughts, Benjie's parents returned home, holding each other tightly. For days after, the village was filled with the endless chatter of its inhabitants. They began to concoct stories to account for the strange goings-on that had transpired, to attempt to answer the questions which so perplexed them. Benjie's disappearance and Honesto's silence gave them much to discuss, and they spent themselves in the task as if throwing lumber to feed an ever-growing and ever-greedy fire. Some said the foolish boy had finally gotten the punishment he deserved, that some terrible, yet unknown retribution had been exacted by the Origin Tree itself. Others came to believe that Benjie had never actually climbed after all, that instead he had disappeared, perhaps to mourn his loss, perhaps to start his life anew. And then there was the children's song...

Eventually, inevitably, having exhausted their tongues and ears, one by one they grew silent. And so things went back to the way they had been, and the Origin Tree once again stood undisturbed and unoccupied. Though there had been mutterings concerning punishment, nothing came of it, and Honesto and the other guardians returned to their old responsibilities. Benjie's mother kept to her duties tending to the Origin Tree, though now she brought with her a bowl of fish and rice each night, leaving it there even though the bowl remained full whenever she returned. All about the village, children could be seen climbing the trees surrounding the village, their arms growing larger and stronger by the day.

As for Honesto, he would spend his remaining days, which were many and plentiful, pondering the questions that lingered from his encounter with the woman in the wood, even as his father's boat rocked gently back and forth in time with the sea's unchanging, eternal symphony. When he would go out fishing alone, or when his boatmate had drifted off to sleep, he found himself singing the children's song. Often quietly, barely a whisper. Sometimes louder, accompanied by the drumming of his fingers against the carved wood.

Where are the lovers, where can they be?
The patient husband and his bride-to-be.
She returned for him after months at sea,
And now they sit in the Origin Tree,
In the Origin Tree, where no one can see.

Nothing Like Chongqing
Stephanie Barbé Hammer

Remember the time we visited the university library in Chongqing, and we saw those beautiful dragon manuscripts?

Of course, as non-Mandarin (or Cantonese) speakers, we could not read anything at all. The Chinese orthographic system is so different from English; we could just barely make out the characters for *man, woman* and *exit*, and that after studying with a private tutor for three months before the trip. But we took in the elegant pictures of dragons and we gloried in the roof garden at the top of the library where they served purified hot water and you could look out over the university, then walk down and eat ice cream from jovial vendors on the street.

But you died right after that trip. I had retired from my university job teaching literature so we could travel. But after you died, I had to figure out the finances. They weren't great, I discovered. You shouldn't have died, and I shouldn't have retired.

But I needed to retire to figure that out.

Now, I'm here in this Pacific Northwest American city trying to restart my academic career.

I'm standing at the entrance of a big university campus looking for the library so that I can do research on how to teach something called English Composition.

I hear there are jobs teaching people how to write. Composition is what one studies now that one no longer studies literature. That's what I studied, of course, but there's no time to study things like: Kafka and Chuang Tzu, Pessoa and Beckett, Genet and Sei Shonagon and Roberto Bolaño and all those people who don't train you to be or do something. So, instead of teaching literature, college instructors teach people about all the different ways you can write an essay so you can get a better job in the real world.

The instructor won't get the better job themselves, naturally. But then, teachers never do. Look at Socrates, and Bashō (which means "banana" in Japanese) and that depressing Professor Unrat, as well as all of Philip Roth's professors, and the other professors in literature. They are never successful, except for that one silly man in *White Noise* who wears sunglasses and can't speak German.[1]

So I go to the university library to learn about the vast field of theories and methodologies connected to composition. I feel intimidated. How does one even start with things like "pathways to competencies"?

This campus is intimidating too. It's "ginormous" to use the parlance of our times. I can't see where the library might be, because the parking lot is next to a stadium and that's next to very tall buildings.

Where are you, library? I cry as I walk up to the parking kiosk near the main university bus stop. Here trucks whizz past me, irate with this solitary pedestrian with her blue umbrella and her wrinkles.

"I'm right here, old lady," says a young girl in a red t-shirt inside the kiosk.

I try to stand very tall and hold my chin up which minimizes the facial sag.

The parking kiosk girl scrutinizes me.

"Sorry, I thought for a moment you were old, but you are within the range of acceptability age-wise so I will speak with

---

[1] The other exception might be Master Kang (aka Confucius), but our translator Min Yang thinks he's pretty boring.

you," she pauses, "although I have my doubts that you are as young as your clothes and general attitude say you are."

I shake with fear. To be recognized as part of the ranks of the senior citizenry in this country is dangerous. This means others can actually see that I am one of the people of the diminished capability, the people of the dreaded walkers: the people who – if they are lucky enough and white enough and rich enough – have a foreign person taking care of them, or – if they are themselves foreign (or perceived as foreign [the categories seem to be shrinking]) will have to cope as best they can with the assistance of our ever-disappearing government and ever-weakening family structures.

"I will take care of you, if you come to live in China," my translator Yang Min said to us. "We love old people here."

"That's very nice" I told her. "But it's a problem that you can't drink the water."

"Not as much as you think," she said. "And after all, can you really live in a country where everyone really just wishes you would die?"

I remain silent, as the red-shirted girl in the kiosk thrusts a paper map at me. "There's an app with a map," she says somewhat jauntily (perhaps aware of the prosody of her phrasing?). "But you people can't understand those, so take this."

"There are four libraries, and—" then she mutters their names and points vaguely down an enormous hill.

Red Square, I think she says, so I gather my courage and reply gamely, "you mean like Tiananmen?"

"Will there be a picture of Mao in the center?"

She looks at me sharply.

"Hey – are you one of those escapees from the facility down the street? We get them all the time." She talks louder. "Do you know your own name, lady?" she says. "Or do I need to call the police?"

"No," I say quickly. "I do NOT have dementia. I just thought..." And then I realize I can't explain how I've been to China but not to Russia, which is where my actual family is from, and where – there really IS a Red Square.

"I was making a little historical political joke," I clarify and smile charmingly, showing my white and quite youthful looking teeth. "About the color red and its connection to old-time communism."

"Communism?" she says. "What's that?"

"Thanks," I say and leave before she can telephone someone to come get the secretly old lady. I try not to shuffle but to stride the way young confident people do.

Remember this at all costs, older people and particularly women: walk with confidence and swing your arms. It makes you look younger.

Then I think of something else I've just noticed: the parking girl's lunch sitting on the kiosk ledge – two smashed Power Bars and a banged-up plaid thermos. WORK-STUDY it reads on the side of the thermos, in capital letters.

Oh yes, I think. She has to work that job to pay for school.

Before I retired from teaching literature, a tall boy yelled at me from the back of the classroom: "What are we supposed to DO when we graduate? How are we supposed to pay off our loans?"

I couldn't answer those questions.

I still can't.

With my new found (still somewhat fearful) empathy, I attempt to stride away from the kiosk until the underpaid parking girl (who is perhaps a student in Communications or Business or some real-world-based major where they promise but can't deliver a career that helps you pay the rent and purchase health insurance even though you have indeed SUCCESSFULLY completed two courses in Composition) can't see me anymore, and then I start shuffling because no one is paying attention. I open my umbrella against the snow, and I amble down the hill to the aforementioned Red Square.

The library in question has huge steps. I can barely flex my knees enough to clear the rises.

I enter. All I see at first is an enormous auditorium filled with coffee machines and sandwiches.

No books anywhere. Which seems ironic.

I walk up and down more stairs. The ceiling gapes above me, and I see the third flight of steps – a grand staircase, made of marble with an enormous bannister, so thick it would take a giant's hand to put their palm across it.

THIS WAY TO THE THIRD FLOOR reads a sign.

What about the second floor? I wonder.

I walk down.

Ah. The room of computers. Banks of them with placards on top.

To be used only by patrons and those with the proper identification.

I open my purse and pull out my driver's license, a coffee gift card with a lot of money still on it, receipts for places I've travelled in China. And the address of our translator. And her phone number too.

"Should you ever come back," Yang Min said.

I scan the room. There are shadows, very slim, and from their rapidity, I suspect youthful; they flutter through the area. Finally, one of them pauses, and becomes a man in black shorts.

Shorts? It's snowing outside. These Pacific Northwest people – they baffle me.

I look at him and he bends over, his beard growing and turning grey, til he looks almost as old as me. But he isn't. He's just one of the poor young people, scratching out an existence in this dot com city.

His t-shirt has a hole in it. He is grasping an enormous black canister out of which a quite good coffee aroma erupts.

"Can I help you?" he says. He pauses and then looks at me more closely.

"How old are you?"

I take a step backwards.

Again with this terrifying question.

My masquerade must be failing. Generally I manage the business of "looking younger than my age" with care and attention.

My regime:

Every day, I apply my mask of moisturizer and apply the oil that renders my hair apparently lustrous and flexible. The body is a bigger challenge, but I manage even that sometimes. I managed it today, perhaps until the snow and rain came.

"What are you dreaming about?" says the poor young librarian man with the beard and the black shorts and his canister of admittedly pretty good-smelling coffee.

"I'm dreaming about your holdings," I lie.

"Do you need a web ID?" he is getting impatient.

I think of duck feet and shudder *no* and say, "I just want to look at the books."

He shrugs.

"Then use this public computer here for seniors." He points.

That computer is older and bigger and it boasts a sad little kitchen stool instead of a chair.

The keys are so worn down I can hardly read the letters, but since I am an excellent typist I manage ok.

Composition Pedagogy I type.

But because it's such a depressing topic, I also type:

Fairytales
Melancholy
Hot Water

I find the call numbers, but there is no directory telling me what books are where. I look around. The young shadows dart back and forth holding tablets and devices.

I decide to brave the giant staircase.

A third of the way up, my way is blocked by a woman in a green evening gown, her dress arranged over the steps, and two men – one with a camera, and the other with a hamburger – telling her how to look so that people will buy the dress.

"Excuse me," I say. They won't move, so I begin folding myself up into compartments.

I learned how to self-fold when I interned at Bloomingdales long ago.

Folding myself up in order to sell perfume, is why I went into academics. I didn't want to have to market anything, but gosh was that naïve. As it turned out, I had to fold myself up a lot at the university. *Please take our major, please get our PhD.* Near the end of my tenure, our Dean made us go door to door dressed in our academic regalia in order to ask for money for scholarships. And then fold ourselves up before the eyes of the homeowner. A circus trick. It worked sometimes.

I have folded myself up to the size of a generously sized diploma, but I still can't squeeze by the model and the men.

"You'll have to get smaller, ma'am," says the guy with the burger who must be the director because he is so imperious. "We won't yield to you. This is an important photoshoot."

I do another set of folds and slip past them. I almost trip over a coke can that is standing next to the burger man.

There is a bag of French fries next to that. I cough loudly and bend over.

I grab the bag with a tiny origami hand.

I clear the step.

I unfold myself and lumber up the rest of the stairs.

The third floor has a landing covered with photographs of white men.

Ah yes. The Founders.

Now I enter a room with long tables and lamps under a vaulted cathedral ceiling, equipped with stained-glass windows.

Victor Hugo would like it.

The wooden tables gleam, and all along the walls are actual volumes!

But, sadly, the room is empty except for two women with mops and buckets who are arguing in different languages with a man with glasses.

"Calm down," he keeps on telling them in English, waving a lanyard with an ID card on it. "Use the Windex and then the Murphy's Oil. And hurry. There's a lot to do."

I hear them sigh as I take out my piece of paper with the call numbers of the books I want on them. I try to match the numbers up with the books here on this floor.

Wait – there are no numbers on these volumes! The books are just here as decoration.

"Where are the PQ's?" I ask the cleaning women.

"We don't have time to read," says one in perfect English. "We are just in the business of cleaning. Don't bother us, old woman."

I feel my face. Yes, the moisturizer has worn off.

The second one whispers, "Do you have a pension?"

"Yes," I whisper back. "But it isn't nearly enough."

"Get back to work," says the supervisor.

I look for a way out of the room that doesn't take me past the plaques of white men. They depress me.

"Which is more crucial to survival?" Yang Min asked me as we crossed a busy Chongqing street. "Water or affective attention?"

Now a dumb waiter opens in the wall of decorative books, and I crawl into it. I pull my umbrella and my French fries in after me.

I push the one button and hope for the best.

I do actually go down!

I'm on the elusive second floor!

The PQ's are there and so are the PR's – which is lucky. I find three books. I sit at a desk and start to read them.

But all I can think about now is how I miss China. We had such a good time there.

Remember the noodles? Remember the bookstore where you could not find Mao's little red book, although you looked all over?

I begin eating the French fries. I turn the pages.

It's no good.

I stand up at my desk.

I cannot spend the rest of my life pretending to be young and traipsing through meaningless research venues. I loved teaching but I do not know how to teach people how to write essays about why they are perfect for the job in question.

Do I summon a dragon?

No.

I become one.

"Can I go where you're going?" says the second cleaning lady, who appears by the desk as I begin to scale over – which is quite a scratchy, though agreeable, sensation.

She says her name is Amarantha.

"Like in Marquez's novel?" I say gruffly, trying not to overturn the desk with my rapidly expanding wings.

I start to explain but she looks impatient.

"Just because I work with my hands doesn't mean I don't know things," she says. "*100 Years of Solitude*. Duh."

I finish transforming, and she climbs aboard with the mop.

I prepare to soar.

"Wait!" shouts Amarantha into my well-shaped ear. "Who's that?"

I look down my long snout and there's the parking kiosk girl with her red t-shirt. She's looking up at me, clutching her thermos and books.

Actual books. Codices.

"I don't have enough money to pay tuition," she says. "I want to come too!"

"Being a foreigner is not easy," I warn her.

"It can't be any harder than it is here," she says, clambering aboard with her copies of *The Book of Disquiet* and *The Journey to the West.*

"I'll take care of us," Amarantha reassures the t-shirt girl. "After all, I speak the international language of cleaning."

Before I break into the ceiling I apologize to t-shirt girl for making an obscure joke about communism, and she apologizes to me for accusing me of being elderly.

"But I AM ELDERLY!" I roar proudly for the first time ever as we tear through the roof (it needed retiling).

We fly away.

Perhaps to Chongqing.

Or perhaps to some even more voluminous city with skyscrapers and tea houses by the river. Perhaps there is a library there that floats above the city. Where you can find all the hardcopy books you like, with floor plans leading in multiple directions. With many ways in and out and around.

Perhaps I'll see you right there next to me in the library garden, and you'll be holding a cup of hot water in one hand, and in the other the ice cream from the street vendor who laughed when you tried to tell her in halting Mandarin, "We are American." To which she answered, "I am Chinese."

You'll tell that story to our group and we'll all chortle at the memory. Yang Min will remind us that in China it is polite to state the obvious, as Amarantha and the parking kiosk girl begin composing poems about sanitation and vehicles. Then we'll notice for the first time how the characters of the Chongqing dragon manuscripts are almost legible, as Yang Min translates, her young voice ringing like a bell.

But somewhere in the distance I hear another bell ringing. I walk back inside and follow the sound down a hallway and poke my head in through an open door. There the students sit, young and old, big and small. Some are speaking Chinese, and some are speaking English, and some are speaking languages I don't yet know. They turn towards and I walk right in and sit with them at one of the little tables – not at the front because that creates too much distance – and I start immediately speaking about the beauty of writing.

They nod and listen. But then they interrupt.

Teach us, Teacher! they all cry suddenly. *Teach us composition.* And although I am used to thinking about literary genres, I turn my mind to templates of opinion: how to agree, disagree, or agree partially. How to structure citing your evidence.

It's like a foreign language, I tell them. *Aristotle called it Rhetoric.* They start taking notes tapping on devices. I look down at the trim textbook as the words compress themselves, getting ready to fly off the page.

My Mother/My Coach
Martin H. Levinson

When I was ten I had a batting slump. No matter how hard I tried I was not able to hit a rubber Spalding ball with a wooden stickball bat. I became an easy out for the pitcher and as a result I was the last person chosen to be on a team in the street pick-up games that my friends and I looked forward to after school each day.

Stickball was the most important part of my life in the nineteen-fifties, and my poor performance made me miserable. I couldn't concentrate on my schoolwork, I couldn't enjoy TV, I couldn't eat. I thought myself a totally worthless human being. I longed for the two-sewer shots I had always been able to thump out, the solid line drives that careened off parked cars, and the adulation of my ball-playing buddies. But I just couldn't hit.

One day, as I lay sobbing on my bed thinking about my failed athletic prowess, my mother walked through the door and asked, "What's the matter?" I could barely get the words out through my tears. "I'm in a batting slump. I can't hit. I'm washed up. No one wants me on their team. I wish I was dead."

She gave me a "mother will make it all better" look and then she said, "Everyone has slumps. Your father has times when he's not very effective at the office. I have weeks when it's tough for me to accomplish what I want to do. Even God isn't perfect. The trick is to keep on going and not get down on yourself."

Her supportive words boosted my sagging spirits but her offer to pitch sock balls to me across the living room floor saved my life. For one week, in the late afternoon before my father came home from work, my mother threw rolled up balls of socks to me in the living room, which I tried to hit with my stickball bat. To my surprise, I was able to smash those sock balls with complete authority. Lamps fell, the aerial was knocked off the TV, and knick-knacks went flying every which way, as my batted sock balls found their marks. My mother said nothing about the damage I was causing. Instead, after each successful whack, she shouted, "good hit" or "excellent shot." My self-confidence soared. By the following the week I was once again slamming two-sewer blasts and my stickball chums were picking me first in the choose-up games on our block.

Some adults have fond memories of the toys their parents gave them or the trips they took them on. I barely remember those things. My fondest childhood memory is my 5'2" mother, who knew next to nothing about sports, pitching easy to hit sock balls and encouraging words to a distraught, stressed-out kid in a cramped, pre-war Brooklyn apartment house.

Light Traveler

Kareem Tayyar

I

I'd always wanted to hitchhike. Ever since Soha and I saw *It Happened One Night* on television the summer we were sixteen, both of us taking turns pretending to be Claudette Colbert lifting up her skirt to show a little thigh. But by the time I was old enough to have done it, the war had broken out, and we were, like everyone else in Beirut, living in near permanent lockdown. One no longer fantasized about hitchhiking. One longed to go to the supermarket without getting blown up; one dreamed of fleeing the country entirely.

It was five years later when, after ten months spent sleeping on the floor of my cousin Leyla's apartment in the Bronx, that I shoved my clothes, paints, and sketchpad into my duffel, locked the door behind me, walked downstairs, and put my thumb in the air. There would be no leg baring for me; it was only early April, which meant, for a girl used to the warm Lebanese climate, it seemed colder than the planet Hoth in *The Empire Strikes Back*. Instead I was decked out in my usual uniform: blue jeans, black sweater, and the black combat boots my father had given me – the man still wishing for a son until the day I left – as a going-away gift. I looked like a starving poet, right down to my split ends and chewed-fingernails. Jack Kerouac would have loved me; Ginsberg too, if he had swung the other way.

II

I was somewhere outside of Portsmouth Ohio, and the man who had picked me up an hour earlier, a trucker named Delon whose Yankees baseball hat had been a pleasant surprise, was telling me about the region's history.

"This used to be Underground Railroad Territory. Escaped slaves would swim the Ohio River and vanish upon reaching the other side."

Through the window was nothing but highway, telephone wire, and two white crosses just off the road. I thought of Walker Evans, of Robert Frank's *The Americans*, of Bruce Springsteen, whom an older cousin had turned me onto.

"My mother escaped from Syria when she was eleven years old," I said. "Her parents put her in the trunk of a neighbor's car, and he drove her across the border in the middle of the night."

Delon looked at me for a moment before looking back to the road.

"One of these days hopefully everyone can stop running."

"Come on, Delon. You know how *Bonnie and Clyde* turns out."

"How long did you say you'd been in America?"

"Less than a year."

"Then how come you talk like Humphrey Bogart's little sister?"

"My father was obsessed with American culture," I said. "Jazz music, the Big Red Machine, Eliot Ness, *Self-Reliance*, the Grateful Dead. All of it."

Delon shook his head and laughed, just as he had when I'd approached him at a Union 76 Station in Harrisburg and asked if he was headed west.

"Are you religious, Delon?"

"There's no such thing as a trucker who isn't."

"How come?"

"Because a long-hauler spends his life being given too far to drive in too little time, yet he always believes he'll make it with room to spare. If that's not faith, then I don't know what is."

"You sound like my grandfather. He thinks God is waiting for him at the breakfast table every morning."

We slowed to let a herd of elk cross the highway. They looked like creatures from another universe.

"You don't?" Delon asked.

"No. Not anymore. Actually I'm not sure I ever did."

"You've got to believe in something."

"Monet," I said.

"Monet? Is he the one that cut his own ear off?"

"No. That was Van Gogh."

"Which one was Monet?"

"He liked to paint waterlilies. Big, colorful ones."

"Listen, you be sure to paint one of those and send it to me when you get to L.A."

"You got it, Delon," I said.

III

I entered Indiana in the backseat of a Camaro that belonged to two sisters who were on their way to Milwaukee to visit their dying father. When we stopped for dinner in a diner where the jukebox played nothing but Elvis Presley, I ordered two cheeseburgers and the largest glass of beer I'd ever seen. We slid into an oval-shaped booth whose seat cushions had begun to tear. Outside a young boy swung a baseball bat at an imaginary fastball, while his mother filled their sedan with gasoline.

"What's in Chicago?" the older sister, Laurie, pushing 40, whose peroxide blonde hair fell across her Doobie Brothers concert t-shirt, asked.

"There's a painting I want to see," I said.

"Long way to go for a painting," she said.

"Which one?" the younger one, Betsy, 35 or so, whose sandy blonde hair featured bangs that made her look like one of Charlie's Angels, asked.

"*Nighthawks*," I said. "By a guy named Edward Hopper."

"Is is pretty?" Betsy asked.

"In a lonely sort of way," I answered.

"I hate feeling lonely," Betsy said.

"That's because you need to find a man," Laurie said.

"Who says you can't be lonely with a man?" Betsy answered.

"You see what I'm dealing with here?" Laurie said, looking at me and smiling.

The waitress, an attractive blonde about Betsy's age, brought our food.

"Can I get you anything else?" she asked.

"This one needs a man," Laurie said, pointing at Betsy.

"Arcadia's," she said, without hesitation. "You'll see it a few miles before you get to Indianapolis."

"What's Arcadia's?" Laurie asked, her eyes widening.

"You'll see," the waitress said, winking.

We had another few hours of hard driving. Nothing beyond the windows to look at other than tall grass and burnt rubber. One billboard warning of the coming apocalypse; another promising salvation to those willing to repent.

"Look," I said, leaning in between the front seats and pointing at a neon sign that featured the silhouette of a shirtless man in a bowtie.

"Oh hell yes," Laurie said.

"I don't believe it," Betsy said.

"God Bless America," I said.

Inside there were strobe lights, there were waitresses in high heels and feathered boas, there was rock-and-roll music playing at ear-splitting decibels.

The men onstage wore bowties and and black g-strings. They had dark tans and defined muscles. They were the kind of men who made me temporarily forget about wanting to see the Pacific Ocean.

"I told you that you needed a man," Laurie shouted over the music.

"No," Betsy shouted back. "I needed *these* men."

We took a seat at a table against the eastern wall of the club. One of the men spotted us, leapt from the stage, and strutted over, his footsteps perfectly in time to the drumbeat. He sat on Betsy's lap, wrapped his legs around her, and began to thrust. Betsy shrieked with joy. Laurie slapped his butt. I calculated exactly how many miles I was from home.

Three hours later we were standing in the parking lot behind the club, waiting for our ears to pop. Laurie was smoking a cigarette. Betsy was nursing a beer. I kept thinking about one of the dancers, a brunette with a swimmer's body. I imagined all the different poses I wanted him to hold.

"I think I'm drunk," I said.

"They have beer where you're from?" Betsy asked.

"It isn't outer space," I said.

"It looks like it on the news sometimes," Laurie said.

"Yes," I admitted. "It does."

We slept that night in a motel whose wallpaper was striped like a carnival tent.

"If I kill one of you in your sleep tonight," Laurie said. "The wallpaper made me do it."

Late the next morning we said our goodbyes in front of the Art Institute.

"You sure you guys don't want to come in to see the painting?" I asked.

"It's better in my imagination," Laurie said.

"Send us a postcard," Betsy added. "You have our address."

IV

For years I had identified with the lone woman in the painting, whose red hair and even redder dress made her look like the kind of vixen who wouldn't be afraid of anything: not living in a Middle Eastern war-zone, not hitchhiking across a country she wasn't familiar with.

But standing in front of it, I felt like the lone man in the fedora whose face is hidden from view. He seems to be in his own world, while the other three appear to be in conversation. What was his story? I wondered. Was there anyone waiting for him at home? Was he not going home? Was he thinking about leaving his wife? His mistress? Was he a cop? A criminal? Was he tired of being the Man in the Gray Flannel Suit? Or was he mourning the fact that he'd never be the Man in the Gray Flannel Suit?

I was in Des Moines by late afternoon; Lincoln, Nebraska by early evening. In between I'd bummed rides from a man who wanted to know if Jesus Christ was my Lord and Savior, and another who tried to give me the pistol he kept in his glove compartment before I stepped out of the car.

I rode with three college girls who played The Rolling Stones at top volume and offered me a joint while they sang along to the radio. I liked the ballads; they loved the fast songs.

By the time I checked into a roadside motel an hour outside of Lincoln, I realized I'd gotten food poisoning at the last place I'd eaten. I spent the next thirty-six hours feeling sick and watching television. There were hostages being held by Iranian gunmen wearing masks; there was a curly-haired tennis player yelling at the line judge; there was word that gay men were dying of pneumonia for mysterious reasons.

Somewhere around 9pm *To Catch a Thief* came on.

I fell asleep dreaming of stealing diamonds with Cary Grant.

I woke up in the middle of the night feeling better than I had in weeks. Which is something I'm guessing no one in Room 217 of the Starlight Lodge in rural Nebraska, had ever said. I undressed, wrapped myself in the spare towel that sat on the bathroom sink, and slipped quietly through the gates of a pool that looked cleaner than I had thought it would be.

I hadn't seen that many stars since one night in Tannourine when my family and I had gone camping the spring before the war broke out. Even the river had smelled like cedars.

I was never the swimmer that my mother had been, but I moved through that over-chlorinated water like a poor man's mermaid. With no light coming from any of the windows, and not a single car speeding by on the highway, I felt as if I were floating at the very edge of the world.

An hour later I stepped from the water, wrapped the towel around me, and walked back to the room. After the kind of warm, luxurious shower I no longer afford myself–I have become an almost embarrassingly devout conservationist–I dressed in my other pair of jeans, my other dark sweater and, with my hair still wet, walked out onto the highway and in the direction of the roadside diner whose neon sign burned bright enough to let drivers know they never closed.

Inside there was a couple draped across one another in a booth towards the back. The boy looked like he had just stepped out of a John Mellencamp song; the girl looked like she hated her father. There was a rotating pie rack with no pies in it; there was a waitress who looked like my grandmother.

The waitress walked over to take my order. "Martha" was written on her name-tag.

"What are you doing out at this time of night?" she asked, just like my grandmother would have.

"I couldn't sleep."

"That's why I work this shift," she said, commiserating. "I can't either."

"What's the best thing you've got here?"

"The fried chicken. It comes with mashed potatoes that'll make you think you're back on the farm."

"I've never been on a farm."

"I realized it the moment I said it. Where you from, honey?"

"Lebanon."

"I've never been there."

"It's beautiful. At least it used to be."

"I know the feeling," she said.

"But this is a gorgeous country," I said.

"Sometimes it is," she said. "More often it's not."

She turned and walked back into the kitchen to place my order. The cook, a man even older than she was, poked his head out from the back and looked in my direction. I waved; he nodded.

A few minutes later she came out with the food. The couple in the back booth had fallen in and out and back into love in the time between my order and its delivery.

"I didn't catch your name, honey," she said, putting the plate in front of me.

"Nour," I said.

"It's lovely. What does it mean?"

"Light," I said, taking a bite of the potatoes.

"What did I tell you?" she asked.

"I think I've found Heaven."

"And here I thought it was Nebraska," she said. "Where you headed?"

"Los Angeles."

"You'll be near the ocean."

"That's the plan."

"It's a good one," she said.

I finished the food so quickly that she came back to my table concerned.

"It isn't good to eat so fast, honey."

"I couldn't help it," I said, seeing that the cook had poked his head out from the back again.

"You hear that," she said loudly, turning to him. "You've got yourself a fan."

This time he smiled at me, waved.

"He lost most of his hearing in the war," she said. "A bomb went off not five feet from him."

I thought of my nephew, Adnan, who'd lost his right foot when he stepped on a land-mine while walking home from school.

"It never stops, does it?" I asked.

"No, honey. It never does."

I paid my check and pocketed the receipt and was heading towards the door when she emerged from the kitchen with a paper sack.

"Take this," she said. "It'll keep."

"I can't."

"Yes," she said. "You can."

I was back in the motel room and getting ready for bed when I looked inside. There was a tupperware container full of mashed potatoes, and another full of fried chicken wings.

There was also a small envelope with my name misspelled on the outside.

Inside was a military necklace with a soldier's information written on it:

Private Steven Terrell

22nd Infantry

Protestant

There was a short note written on the back of the receipt.

He'd always wanted to be buried at sea. But this will have to do.

Have a good life, honey.

I slipped the necklace over my head, and fell asleep with the coolness of the metal slowly warming against my body.

V

I was just inside the Colorado state line, finishing off the last of the chicken when the car pulled up to the side of the road, and a woman about my age, a sandy blonde with glasses and a laminated photograph of Glen Campbell dangling from the rearview mirror, smiled, and said,

"I might be the only car you see for hours."

I threw my duffel in the back seat, and pulled the handle of the passenger side door.

"You've got to yank it," she said. "It's stubborn that way."

Once in, we tore down Route 76 at a rate of speed faster than which I was comfortable. The radio station was playing a country song about a guy whose best friend had died in Vietnam. I fingered the necklace, and thought about my mother.

"I thought Colorado would be prettier than this," the driver, whose name was Jennifer, said.

"Maybe further on," I offered.

"Maybe," she agreed, before turning down the volume on the radio. "What are you doing on the road?"

"I'm headed to Los Angeles."

"Me too."

"Really?"

She nodded.

"I've got a friend I can stay with out there. She lives on Sunset Boulevard."

We passed a truck stop with a giant Confederate flag painted on the side of the building.

"I thought I'd seen the last of those once I got out of Arkansas," she said.

I rolled down the window and felt the wind run through my hair. The clouds looked like a fleet of magic carpets. Over the course of the next two hours Jennifer told me her story. It was the same one that every woman in every country on earth has heard so many times it's as familiar to them as the scent of her own skin. The only details that change are the names of the men.

"I figured if I didn't go now, then I never would."

I thought of my parents telling me they were too dug in to leave, and of my friends who said they'd rather die on their own land than live on someone else's.

I thought of the way the country you love can become like a man who believes you don't have the courage to leave him.

"What are you going to do when you get to L.A.?" she asked.

"I don't know. Whatever I have to."

"That's a dangerous thing to say, where we're going."

"You're right," I said. "I take it back."

We laughed, and slipped into silence for a few minutes before Jennifer broke it by asking,

"What do you miss most about home?"

"The movie theater a couple of blocks from where I grew up," I said.

"What was it called?"

"The Poet's Castle. They burned it down on a Saturday night. On Sunday morning I knew I was leaving."

Jennifer, trying to steer the conversation back to happier ground, asked,

"Do you have a favorite?"

"Favorite what?" I asked.

"Film," she said, before adding, "Mine's *Barefoot in the Park*. You ever seen that one?"

"Of course," I said. "With Robert Redford. My girlfriends were all in love with him."

I paused, and considered what to put at the top of my list.

"*Casablanca*, I guess," I said.

"That's such a sad one!" Jennifer said. "I like ones with happy endings."

"My mother feels the same way. She wasn't the same for a month after we saw *Love Story*."

"I agree with your mother," she said. "There's enough sadness in the real world already. I don't need movies to remind me of that."

We pulled into a gas station a few years past being a few years past its prime.

"Do those pumps even work?" Jennifer asked.

While I filled up the tank Jennifer went inside to buy a soda and a pack of gum. I squeezed my finger to the trigger of the pump and watched the numbers whirl like cherries on a slot machine.

He was standing at the edge of the road, about twenty yards away from the car. He wore a black shirt and faded blue cargo pants. He looked to be in his late 30s, with dark skin and salt-and-pepper hair.

When Jennifer came back out she saw what I was looking at.

"Exactly," she said.

"I didn't say anything."

"You didn't have to, honey," she said. "You think we should pick him up?"

"It isn't my decision," I said. "But I think we should pick him up."

"I always knew you were smart."

His name was Thomas. Up close he had a thin scar along the side of his jaw, and the bluest eyes I'd ever seen.

Back out on the road Jennifer looked into the rearview mirror and asked,

"You just get out of the Army or something?"

"Or something," he said. "The Merchant Marines."

"How long were you in?" I asked.

"Too long," he said.

"Where are you headed?" Jennifer asked.

He smiled, warmed up.

"Home. Utah."

"They've got the Salt Lake, don't they?" Jennifer asked.

"They do," he said. "But that's a long way from where I'm going."

"You're Native American," I said.

"You're not," he answered, smiling.

"No," I said.

"Where are you from?"

"Beirut."

"I was in Tripoli about eighteen months ago. You were smart to leave."

"What were you doing there?" Jennifer asked.

"Making deliveries," he said, before immediately changing the subject. "I didn't know if people still picked up hitchhikers anymore."

"They don't," Jennifer said. "I'm the last one."

"Is that true?" he asked, looking at me.

"Not exactly," I said. "But close enough."

An hour later we were driving through a fog so thick we couldn't see five feet in front of us. We were in a forest of some sort, or at least we had been a few minutes earlier, before the fog had descended.

"Now I know what Little Red Riding Hood felt like," he said.

"Let's hope we have better luck than she did," I said.

"Cut it out, you two," Jennifer said. "I'm scared enough as it is."

"You want me to drive?" he asked.

"I've come all this way without a man taking the wheel," Jennifer said. "I'm not going to stop now."

"Fair enough," he said, holding up his palms in surrender.

I rolled down the window.

"I hear music," I said.

"I hear it too," Jennifer said.

The music was loaded with enough strings to make me wonder if we had died in a car accident and angels had come down with their violins to guide our spirits to Paradise.

"I know that voice," he said, a minute later, when dialogue had replaced the music.

"Who is it?" Jennifer asked.

"Orson Welles," I said.

"I don't know who that is," Jennifer said.

"*Citizen Kane*," he said.

"I've never seen that one," Jennifer said.

"You wouldn't like it," I said.

"How come?" she asked.

"He dies in the end," I said.

"You know who never dies at the end of his movies?" she said.

"Who?" I asked, already starting to laugh.

"Burt Reynolds."

"She has a point," Thomas said.

We followed the sound for a few more minutes, before turning onto a small road and beginning to move into a valley where the fog slowly dissipated. There was an enormous screen rising above a sprawling lot full of parked cars. Here and there waitresses moved in between the sedans, delivering popcorn and sodas. Two young boys played tag near the concession stand.

"My God," Thomas said. "I haven't seen a movie in years."

"How long has it been?" I asked.

"When did *Jaws* come out?"

"That was five years ago!" Jennifer exclaimed, as she maneuvered onto the thin lane that led to the entrance.

"There aren't a lot of movie theaters in the middle of the ocean," Thomas said.

"Now I see you why you left," Jennifer said.

"Exactly," he joked. "It's the reason I gave when I turned in my resignation."

Ten minutes later we were eating hamburgers and watching the final minutes of the film. Welles was chewing scenery like a man who hadn't eaten in weeks.

"I just remembered I hate this movie," Thomas said.

"But it's a classic," I said.

"So is *The Wizard of Oz*," he said. "And I hate that one too."

"How come?" Jennifer asked, grabbing some of my French fries.

"Because we're supposed to feel sorry for a rich white guy who has wrecked his life. And the lives of those around him."

I saw where he was going; Jennifer still seemed to be working through it.

"What do you mean?"

"I mean ask the Vietnamese if they think Richard Nixon is a tragic figure, or whether they think he's a monster who should have had his heart removed from his body without anesthesia."

"I wish somebody would have done that to my husband," Jennifer said.

By the time the next picture – *Singin' in the Rain* – had begun, I found myself wishing my father could have been there to see me, watching a movie in an outdoor theater that no one was interested in burning to the ground.

"Now this is a great movie," Thomas said.

"I've never seen this one either," Jennifer said.

"They show any films in the South besides Burt Reynolds ones?" he asked.

"Careful," she said. "Utah's a long walk from here."

Twenty minutes later Jennifer was sleeping so soundly that I wondered what kind of noises she might sleep through.

"She'd do well in a war-zone," I said.

"Better than I did."

"You were in Vietnam?"

"Unfortunately."

"You were lucky to have survived."

"I could say the same thing about you," he said.

"What are you going to do now?"

He shrugged his shoulders.

"The truth is I have no idea. Maybe teach school."

"What would you teach?"

"Anything. Literature, History, Art."

"Art?" I asked, excited. "Do you paint?"

"That and books were the only things that kept me sane on the ship."

"What do you like to paint?"

"I'm partial to nude women," he said, smiling.

"I bet you are," I said, smiling back.

Jennifer suddenly came to, as if someone had injected a syringe full of adrenaline directly into her heart.

"I just had the craziest dream," she said, looking up as the screen just as Gene Kelly began to swing around a light-pole in the rain.

"What was it?" I asked.

"I was standing alone on a beach in California, and when I stepped out onto the water, I didn't sink."

"So you're Jesus when you dream," I said.

"Is that sacrilegious?" she asked.

"Only if you were wearing a bikini while you did it," I said.

"Ok, good," she said. "Because I was in a one-piece."

"Thank God," I said. "That was a close one."

"You're teasing me," she said.

"Just a little," I answered.

We crossed the Utah state line late the next morning and, a few miles later, pulled into the bus station where Thomas could catch a ride home to his reservation. We parked, got out of the car, and looked towards a blue sky that featured a bright sun and a thin, white, communion wafer of a moon. It looked like something Ansel Adams would have photographed.

"Do they know you're on your way?" Jennifer asked, brushing the crumbs of the chocolate chip cookies the three of us had shared for breakfast off her blouse.

"No," Thomas said. "I stopped writing a few years back."

"They're going to be so happy to see you," Jennifer said.

"I hope so," he said, stepping forward to give her a hug.

Tears filled the corners of Jennifer's eyes, and she started to laugh in embarrassment.

"Sorry," she said to both of us, squeezing him. "I'm a crier."

"There are worse things to be," he said, kissing her on the cheek.

Afterwards Thomas turned to me and said,

"You're going to like Los Angeles."

"How do you know?"

"Because film is a religion there. The only one, actually."

"That sounds lovely," I said, as we began to embrace.

"I'll send you a painting some time," he said.

"I only like male nudes."

"I'll make it a self-portrait then."

"I'll be waiting."

"This is awkward," Jennifer said.

He turned towards the station. He walked with the casual swagger of a man comfortable in his own skin and, when he passed a telephone pole a few feet from the entrance, he swung around it once, and then a second time, before kicking up his heels and vanishing into the building.

"Gene Kelly, eat your heart out," I said.

"You got that right," Jennifer agreed.

The rest of Utah, all of Nevada, and most of California passed in something like a waking dream, a sprawling montage of cows, Mormon temples, stunning rock formations, Christian churches, trailer parks, stray dogs, blown-out tires, adult bookstores, rundown roadhouses, cheap motels, and so many stars that I wondered who on earth had had the time to name them all.

Even now, I can remember the gas station where the owner's wife gave us slices of homemade blackberry pie and refused to take any money for it; I can remember the man who pounded on my passenger window at a stoplight and said he'd kill us if we didn't give him a ride; I can remember that lovely Jehovah's Witness who spread his map on the picnic table outside the pizza place where we'd just eaten and showed us where we were in relationship to Heaven; I can remember those high school kids in East Nevada offering to wash cars for a dollar a piece in order to raise money for a school trip; I can remember that tent city a few miles beyond the Las Vegas city limits that seemed to go on forever; I can remember that great bookstore we stumbled into in Vegas proper, where the old Irishman behind the counter regaled us with stories about Fitzgerald and Hemingway that he'd learned as an assistant editor in New York in the 30s; I can remember the way the sun shone off a rusted water tower a mile past the California state line, lighting it up like an oversized torch.

No Vacancy signs; Jesus Christ for Reagan signs; Gays Repent signs; Rest Stop Ten Miles signs; See the Oldest Dinosaur in the World Signs; Speed Limit 25 signs; Speed Limit 65 signs; signs for cabaret dancers, nickel slots, used cars, fresh pizzas, pre-fab houses, the Runnin' Rebels, *Raging Bull*, Jimmy Carter, Free Credit, No Credit, Pre-Paid Credit, Unlimited Credit...

We took turns driving, we listened to country-and-western, we spilled soda pop on the seats, we peed in bushes off the interstate and prayed that no one could see us...

Wild horses in Cedar City, Veterans for Peace in St. George, low-flying fighter jets in Indian Springs; gunfire in North Vegas; burned hot dogs in Blythe; bighorn sheep in Mojave; abandoned railroad cars in Barstow; dreams of Dust Bowl migrants on Route 66 in Victorville; a night-lit ferris wheel in Pomona that still appears in my dreams, even all these years later...

"Jennifer," I said, nudging her awake.

"What?"

"We're here."

"I don't believe it," she said.

"Look," I said, and pointed to the City Limits sign.

We had more trouble finding the ocean than we had thought we would. The freeways were like a modernist's version of Daedalus' labyrinth, except no goddess had provided thread to help us find our way free. We missed the right onramps, we exited the wrong ones, we kept trying to read a map that looked like the kind of complicated physics equation that Einstein used to spend his free time solving.

But finally, we arrived.

"Whoo whoo!" Jennifer shouted, clapping her hands. "Turn on the radio!"

After we had parked the car on a side street and made our way onto the sand, Jennifer immediately took off her sandals, removed her blouse, slipped out of her blue jeans, and spun two sloppy pirouettes in a bathing suit small enough to have doubled as a leprechaun's handkerchief.

"What on earth?" I asked, laughing.

"I've been waiting for a reason to wear this thing for eight days and five thousand miles," she said. "So no judgement."

"You pull it off," I said. "There's no doubt about that."

As we slowly made our way to the water one couldn't help but people-watch. The scene looked like a cross between Renoir's *The Boating Party* and one of the casino scenes in *Fear and Loathing in Las Vegas*.

We found a space near the shore and took a seat. We looked out at the waves and the surfers riding them. We watched mothers playing in the shallows with children mesmerized by the seashells they found, or who scouted real estate for the best possible place to build a sandcastle. A lifeguard in red trunks and a torso with more than a passing similarity to Michelangelo's David walked by us.

"I think I'm going to like California," I said.

"Oh, honey," Jennifer answered, still looking in his direction. "I already do."

Jennifer was lying on the sand and dozing by the time I rolled my jeans up past my kneecaps, and walked ankle-deep into the water. I looked towards Catalina, and thought it resembled a dragon sleeping off a spell in an ancient folk tale. There were so many other people I wished could have been there with me, with the sun shining above the island like a magic lantern held by a prospecting god who knew he'd struck gold: my mother and father, my brothers and sisters, Delon and Adnan and Martha, Laurie and Betsy, Thomas, the solitary man in *Nighthawks*, the redhead too, and, of course, Steven Terrell, whose dog tags I slipped from around my neck, fingered for a few more moments, and then, wading into deeper water, threw as far as I could into the waves.

ACKNOWLEDGMENTS

So here we are, with the second volume of *The Bridge* after a year's long journey. Despite the current scenario of the pandemic, it is Allah's special benevolence upon us that we've been able to accomplish this goal. The journey was not easy, there were countless obstacles on the way, but praise be to the Almighty, who has ever been very kind. I must also thank the people because of whom I have been able to reach this far. I am highly indebted to my father who has always been there for me with his guidance and advice regarding various issues related to the project. I must also thank my dear mother for her constant prayers and love throughout the way. Whenever I got stuck at some point, her prayers got me out very smoothly. I am also highly obliged to Baba and family for their prayers and good wishes.

At this point I must confess that Volume-II has come out in time just because of my husband, Qasim Nawaz, who has supported me from the beginning and showed his trust in my potential while helping me meet the deadlines. I appreciate all the effort he has put in to make this project possible. I thank him for making the title cover and bearing with my repetitive suggestions for the minuscule modifications in the design. And ofcourse, not to forget the times when he made tea for me when I was busy editing the work.

I am highly indebted to Rehman Faris, my mentor and guide in all creative endeavors, for finding time out of his busy schedule for reviewing the draft of *The Bridge* and writing the foreword for it. I am very obliged to Hasnain Haider Mumtaz for the beautiful calligraphic title that he wrote with his special manuscript pen, giving an absolutely customized look to the cover. I am thankful to my family, specially my nieces for their encouragement and excitement about the project.

The two people without whom this project wouldn't have been completed are Muhammad Saiful Islam and Shannon Phillips. I am extremely thankful to both. To Saif, for introducing me to Shannon, and to Shannon, for offering solution to all issues related to the project by being a perfect guide, editor and publisher all by herself. It was wonderful working with her.

I am obliged to all the writers for their contributions. I am thankful to Prof. Fareeha Basit Khan, the director, Institute of Languages and Culture for paving the way for the project to flourish. Special thanks to all my friends for their support and guidance. In the end, I would like to acknowledge in advance all the readers who are going to read *The Bridge* and contribute in the upcoming volumes.

Aaisha Umt Ur Rashid
Editor from Pakistan

CONTRIBUTORS

Rizwan Akhtar is the Assistant Professor at in the department of English, Punjab University, Lahore, Pakistan. His first collection of poems *Lahore I am Coming* has received tremendous applause in and outside the country. He has also published poems in well-established poetry magazines of the UK, US, India, Canada and New Zealand. He has also done a 5 weeks workshop on poetry with Derek Walcott at the University of Essex in 2010.

Suzanne Allen was born and raised in Southern California, where she now teaches college-level Literature and Writing. Her poems appear in print and online journals and anthologies in five countries, now six, and she has two chapbooks: *verisimilitude* from corrupt press, and *Little Threats* from Picture Show Press. She co-edits *The Bastille* of Spoken Word Paris, and she holds an MFA in Creative Writing from California State University, Long Beach. "912 South Fourth Street, #5" was previously published in *Redshift*.

Lloyd David Aquino teaches composition, literature, and creative writing at Mount San Antonio College. He has published two poetry chapbooks: *Madeline After the Fall* (Arroyo Seco Press) and *Concrete's Song* (Picture Show Press). He is working on a new poetry manuscript and his first graphic novel script.

Zobia Arif is pursuing a bachelor's (Hons) in English Literature from Lahore College for Women University, Lahore, Pakistan. She's been writing poems and short stories since the age of 15. For her, humans are like stories to read hence themes of her works are derived from human nature. Her passion for writing has given her the liberty to colour the world around her with imagination and she uses this power to leave a cathartic impact on her readers.

Stephanie Barbé Hammer is a six time Pushcart Prize nominee. She is the author of a magical realist novel (*The Puppet Turners of Narrow Interior*), a prose poem chapbook (*Sex with Buildings*), a full-length poetry collection (*How Formal?*), and a how-to-write-magical-realism craft book (*Delicious Strangeness*). Stephanie is also Professor Emerita and Distinguished Teacher of Comparative Literature at the University of California, Riverside campus. She has written three scholarly books and more than twenty articles on topics ranging from 18th Century Satire to Octavia Butler's use of food.

Christina Brown holds a master's degree in American Studies from California State University and a bachelor's degree in English from California State University, Channel Islands. She has presented her research at several regional and national conferences, including the California State University Research Competition and the Popular Culture Association conference. Her research focuses include popular culture, gender and technology, storytelling, creative forms, and cultural anxieties. She is also the managing editor at Pear Shaped Press.

Saima Eman is an Assistant Professor at the Department of Applied Psychology at Lahore College for Women University, Pakistan. She has a PhD in Psychology from University of Sheffield, UK. Saima is also a Commonwealth Alumni Advisory Panel Member and Certified Publons Peer Reviewer. She authored a poem in *The Bridge* Volume-I which was published in 2019. She has written more than 100 poems in English and has several published poems in *New Asian Writing, Homec Magazine, poetry.com*, and *Dawn Young World.*

Maania Farhan recently did her master's in Special Education from University of the Punjab, Lahore. She grew up reading mystery thrillers which set her out on an endless journey in a jungle of stories and poetry. She is a short story and poetry writer, and enjoys writing humorous fiction. Her heart is split into two halves, for the love of writing and special education. She lives to see both grow within her and become one someday.

A bureaucrat by profession and a poet by passion, **Rehman Faris** has accomplished amazing feats at quite a tender age. His first collection, *Ishq-Bkhair*, had launch ceremonies in the USA and the UK alike and was received with tremendous warmth. Apart from touching millions of hearts through his fresh craft and fabulous fantasy, Faris has amazed his readers by exhibiting equal grip on as diversified genres as *Marsia, Rubaaiaat*, Poetified travellogues and translations of the global icons of literature to Urdu. Being an anchorperson for television and a columnist for English dailies, Faris has established his God-gifted talent in both the electronic and print media. Arguably the most frequently-quoted poet and the most loved lyricist of the digital/social media generation, he has, until now, performed his recitals in twenty-seven countries; thus making him an internationally sought-after writer.

Brian Harman is the author of *Suddenly, All Hell Broke Loose!!!*, a collection of poems from Picture Show Press. He holds a Master of Fine Arts degree in creative writing from California State University, Long Beach. He is currently working on three collections of poetry, and curating *Poetry Mode*, an online colloquium of all things poetry. His work has been published in *Misfit Magazine, Nerve Cowboy, Pearl*, and elsewhere. His influences include Gerald Locklin, Charles Harper Webb, Prince, and Dadaism.

Mifanwy Kaiser is the founder of Tebot Bach, a community literary organization. She has written poetry since she was in the first grade and used poetry as a teaching tool since 1970. Experienced at working with homeless and prison populations, she currently teaches at Golden West College.

Taha Kehar is a journalist, author and editor. He has served as the head of *The Express Tribune's* Peshawar city pages and was an assistant editor on the opinion's desk of *The News*. A law graduate from SOAS, London, Kehar is the author of two novels, *Typically Tanya* (2018) and *Of Rift and Rivalry* (2014). Kehar's work has been published in *The News on Sunday, South Asia Magazine, The Hindu, The Hindustan Times* and the Delhi-based *Equator Line* magazine. He has also guest-edited *Equator Line's* issue on Pakistani writing. Based in Karachi, he teaches undergraduate media courses and conducts creative writing workshops for young adults.

Judy Kronenfeld is the author of four books of poetry and two chapbooks. Her most recent full-length collections are *Bird Flying through the Banquet* (FutureCycle, 2017) and *Shimmer* (WordTech, 2012). Her poems have appeared in *Cimarron Review, New Ohio Review, Natural Bridge, One (Jacar Press), Rattle, Valparaiso Poetry Review,* and other journals, and in two dozen anthologies. She is Lecturer Emerita, Creative Writing Department, University of California, Riverside, and an Associate Editor of *Poemeleon*. "Voiced and Unvoiced: Resumed Litany for All Language" was first published in *Spoon River Poetry Review*.

Martin H. Levinson is a member of the Authors Guild, National Book Critics Circle, PEN America; the book review editor for *ETC: A Review of General Semantics,* and a contributing editor to *The Satirist.* He has published nine books and numerous articles and poems. He teaches history and foreign policy courses at Stony Brook University (SUNY). Website: martinlevinson.com. "My Mother/My Coach" was first published in *Reflections in Poetry and Prose Vol. 12.*

Nausheen Mazhar is serving as a lecturer of Geography in Lahore College for Women University, Lahore. As a PhD scholar, she has recently availed IRSIP fellowship for School of Earth and Environment, University of Leeds, UK, where she completed her PhD research. She is a poet interested in sensitivity of human life and emotions and her poetry is a pertinent expression of that. She has won various medals and prizes for her literary endeavors and her poetry has been published in local and international forums.

Husnain Haider Mumtaz is a calligraphy artist based in Lahore, Pakistan. He has received a professional diploma in Traditional Arts from National College of Arts, Lahore. His research interests include early *Kufic* writing style of Imam Ali (RA).

Sana Munir, author of *Unfettered Wings: Extraordinary Stories of Ordinary Women* (India; 2018) tells stories of women and her work aims at representation, diversity and acceptance. She believes Feminism enables a person to rid themselves of their gendered lenses. Her book was nominated for Best Fiction (English) at the Valley of Words Literary Festival at Dehra Dun, India. The book was made part of the syllabus of M.Phil students (English Literature) at COMSATS University. Sana was among the top six Pakistani authors by Mashable Pakistan, on Women's Day 2020. Her dissertation of MA (Mass Media Communication), written along the lines of Feminism, was awarded an exceptional score of 99%. It was titled, *Depiction of Women in Disney's Animated Films: The case of the White and Coloured Women.* She has taught Feminist Film Theory, Research Methodology and International Communication at Lahore College for Women, Lahore as an honorary lecturer. Her resume, interviews and book reviews can be accessed at www.sanamunirblog.wordpress.com.

Prof. **Zakia Nasir** is the former Chairperson of English Department, Lahore College for Women University, Lahore. She has 38 years of teaching Literature and language to her credit. She has published poetry in *The Waggle*, an international journal published from Atlanta, U.S. and *The Bridge* (Volume-I). Her first collection of poems is in the process of publication. She is on the editorial board of the Journal of English Language, Literature and Education, Garrison University and Journal of Global Regional Review. Currently she is a visiting faculty for MPhil at LCWU, Garrison University Lahore. "In My Land Lie Embedded My Roots I Have Nurtured Them With My Blood" is a true story, a personal experience. The names and places have been changed for privacy.

Qasim Nawaz is a senior software engineer laden with an extensive experience of software and web development, database administration, graphic designing and freelance e-commerce projects. He has materialized various projects and enterprise level software on national and international levels. He is interested in experimenting with innovative ideas with a blend of creativity and that can be seen in his work. He is the official title cover designer for the project, *The Bridge* and also the motivational force behind it.

Aaisha Umt Ur Rashid is serving as a lecturer of English at Lahore College for Women University, Lahore, Pakistan. She is a poet and short story writer interested in real life stories that happen around her. She has edited, translated and proofread various creative writing projects. *The Bridge* is her recent brainchild. Along with that, her first collection of poems entitled *Miracle of Love* is in the process of compilation.

Iffat Saeed is a Lahore based academician. Her domain is literatures in English language. She has enjoyed a diverse teaching experience at graduate and post graduate level. She believes that her best introduction is the vast student body that she has been privileged to interact with and learn from... an investment of thirty years that has enriched her intellectually and creatively. Translation from Urdu literature into English language remains her favorite preoccupation. In this connection she has had a long association with Academy of Letters and her translations of classic and contemporary literary pieces have featured in many international journals published by the Academy. One of her proud contributions is an article on Professor Mrs. U. Sirajudin published by the Institute for the development of National Language and History entitled Roshni kay Safeer. Her most recent publication is a coffee table book entitled *Three Contemporary Artists*. The book features poems by Yasmeen Hameed and Rizwan Akhtar and is illustrated with miniature works painted by Heera Khan.

Patty Seyburn has previously published five collections of poems, most recently *Threshold Delivery* (Finishing Line Press, 2019). She earned a BS and an MS in Journalism from Northwestern University, an MFA in Poetry from University of California, Irvine, and a PhD in Poetry and Literature from the University of Houston. She is a professor at California State University, Long Beach. www.pattyseyburnpoet.com

Areej Tahir is an aspiring author, driven by the desire to change the world. She started writing at the age of 16, and since then has conjured up poems and short stories about the cruelty on the society. She encourages people to realize that acceptance from society is not the only path they need to tread down upon, and there are many more ways to express themselves. She is currently working on her book, while putting small chunks of her work on websites like Instagram and Wattpad.

Mahnoor Tahir is currently enrolled in MS English Literature program at Lahore College for Women, University. She believes writing is an intrinsic part of her, leading her to participate in various creative writing competitions. She likes to experiment with genres but her play with words remains constant. She firmly believes that writing is a means to express oneself and her writings have been published in the first volume of *The Bridge*.

Kareem Tayyar's novel, *The Prince of Orange County*, is available from Pelekinesis Books, and his new collection of poetry, *Immigrant Songs*, was published by WordTech (2019). A recipient of a 2019 Wurlitzer Fellowship for Poetry, he holds a PhD in American and Poetry Literature from U.C. Riverside and teaches at Golden West College.

Aruni Wijesinghe has taught both English as a Second Language and Dance. She holds a BA in English from the University of California, Los Angeles, an AA in dance from Cypress College and a TESOL certification from the University of California, Irvine. Her work has been published in several journals and anthologies, and more work is forthcoming with *Dryland Literary Journal, Wirecutter Collective, Imagism Gallery* and others. She also serves on the board of directors for Tebot Bach, a community literary organization. "Eating at Home" was first published by Small Fish Big Pond.

ABOUT THE EDITORS

Aaisha Umt Ur Rashid is a poet and short story writer. She is currently serving as a Senior Lecturer in Department of English, Lahore College for Women University (LCWU), Lahore, Pakistan. Having a strong educational background, she has accomplished a bronze medal in Masters (English Literature), and a gold medal in MS (English Literature).

She has effectively initiated the project, *The Bridge* in Pakistan which is a unique venture aiming at connecting writers from across the globe. The first volume, targeting writers from Malaysia, was very successfully published by Silverfish Publishers, Malaysia in 2019, becoming a part of the creative writing courses at IIUM, Malaysia and LCWU, Pakistan. The second volume has brought together writers from America and Pakistan. She aims at bridging bridges with many other countries, bringing writers together on one platform.

She has translated, proofread and edited various creative writing projects. She writes academic and creative articles for diverse blogs, websites and journals. She has been an active participant in numerous Creative Writing projects organized by the British Council. One of the highlights is *The New Silk Road* project held in Dhaka, Bangladesh, where she was one of the five young writers selected from all over the country to represent Pakistan. Presently, she is working on two major projects simultaneously; her own short story collection and compilation of her poems.

She is a member of the Board of Studies at LCWU. She has recently compiled a course book for the BS (English Compulsory) course which will be taught in the coming session. She has also introduced a course titled *Dynamics of Creative Writing* at LCWU. She is looking after the International Collaborations for the department. As Incharge of *Fareeha Basit Khan Literary Society, LCWU*, she organizes various annual and biannual creative and academic events as well as local and international conferences.

Shannon Phillips is the founding editor of *Carnival*, an online literary magazine, which she eventually transitioned into Picture Show Press. She is also the co-founder of the annual Mother's Day poetry reading at Gatsby Books and the recipient of the 28th Moon Prize from *Writing In A Woman's Voice*. Her most recent chapbook, BODY PARTS, was published by dancing girl press. After teaching English as a Second Language and working as admin support in Higher Ed for several years, she decided to take the plunge and become a freelance editor. She holds a Master of Fine Arts degree in creative writing from California State University, Long Beach, as well as an Associate Degree in Arabic from Saddleback College.